BUILDING A STELLAR BUSINESS

A Structured Guide to Financial Success

Michele Johnson &
Lorraine Kennedy

Building a Stellar Business

First published in 2016 by

Panoma Press Ltd
48 St Vincent Drive, St Albans, Herts, AL1 5SJ, UK
info@panomapress.com
www.panomapress.com

Book design and layout by Neil Coe.

Printed on acid-free paper from managed forests.

ISBN 978-1-784520-80-9

A CIP catalogue record for this book is available from the British Library.

This book is available online and in bookstores.

ACKNOWLEDGMENTS

We wish to thank the following people for their help and support, and at times, dripping sarcasm.

Their mentoring, guidance and friendship helped to make this book possible and we could not have done it without them.

Thank you to Scott Brenner, Carole Epstein, Richard Flaskegaard, Miriam Washington Kendall, Mindy Gibbins-Klein, Kip O'Brien, Dr. Dominick Vita and Janet Vita.

And of course, a very special thank you to our children, who make it all so much fun: Christina, Michelle, Clark and Karl.

CONTENTS

INTRODUCTION

This book is actually two books in one.

Chapters 1 - 6 cover the financial structure of your business and the why and how it is vital to your success. It helps you to understand what to look for and what to review, and how to see your business from a financial perspective in order to understand where your profits are currently coming from and to then continue to be successful, financially, going forward.

Chapters 7 - 9 cover other, but equally important, financial aspects of your overall business. These include the importance of structure for your employees in your business, building a strong outside support team and learning to utilize them, and then finally some guidelines for protecting all of your assets.

Our goal was to write a financial reference book that, once read, could then be opened up to any chapter for a quick reread and review.

Chapter 1

A BUSINESS CHECK-UP

STRAIGHT SHOOTING QUESTIONS

Is your business healthy? How do you know? Are your financials accurate and current and do they tell you what you need to know? Do you have a good filing system and know where everything is or are you literally buried in paper? Are you billing and collecting your receivables on a timely basis? Are you protecting your assets? Do you have a good team of professionals to support and help you grow your business? Finally, do you have the right employees, associates and subcontractors working for you?

As financial business consultants, we are often asked by small business owners to provide bookkeeping, CFO and payroll services. We start off with these kinds of questions every time we meet a new client. But actually, one of the first questions we ask is the only question that really matters, the question that really gives you the foundation to start from and to ask all other questions.

ARE YOU MAKING MONEY?

And we usually get one of the following three answers. Answer #1: A resounding "Yes." Great, then we ask: Could you be doing better? Where is the money coming from? Do you understand your profit margins on each of your income streams and thus, do you know where you are making the most money? Are you measuring what you need to measure? And what are you leaving on the table?

Answer #2: Usually accompanied by a sad shake of the head, "No." We ask, are you sure? Maybe you ARE making money and you just don't know it. If the client still thinks that the answer is no, then we ask why not? Do you have a solid financial system that produces a useful set of financial statements every month? Do you have a business plan or forecast to compare it to? Are you billing and collecting on a timely basis? Do you have too much inventory? Do you have too many employees? Is there another cash flow issue?

Answer #3: For many folks it's a most truthful "I don't know." We meet new clients every day who really truly don't know how much money they are making. They seem to have money in the bank and are able to make payroll, but beyond that, they don't know if they are truly making money and where they could make more. They might say that they are working harder than they did last year and still don't see it reflected in the bank. Mostly though, that's why they call us and we need to figure it out together.

Sometimes different variables can turn a No answer into a Yes, or a Yes answer into a No, relatively easily – if you know what you are looking for.

We had a new client who was showing a strong income and good invoicing, but came to find out, he was not paying himself or his wife (who was doing the books). It was more important for him to show profits so he could tell his colleagues at their annual industry meetings than it was to see if he should have been in business in the first place.

We had another new client with good invoicing but not much profit, and waaaay too much inventory. Turns out he wanted to win the vendor's annual sales incentive trip to Italy so he had been over purchasing inventory at the expense of his business.

We received a call from an accountant that we work with who had a client with strong invoicing but much smaller profit than matched their industry. The accountant just figured out that in this case a trusted employee of many years had been stealing from them and could we help them get on the right track.

By bringing in financial professionals to all three of these scenarios, these companies were able to recover and turn around. In these situations our bookkeeping company, Stellar Support Associates, was viewed as a "short term fix" to the problem, with the intent being to turn the books over to another full-time bookkeeping employee. However, the owners quickly realized that they could not afford to hire full-time help at the level of support and knowledge that we were giving them, and that using us was far more economical. All of them went from worrying about making payroll and running to the bank with every check that arrived to being able to plan on expanding their business, hiring more employees (or paying themselves and their spouses!), paying off their line of credit or some combination of the three. They actually started to think about the bottom line operations of the future instead of worrying about today. They went from being REACTIVE in their financial decisions to being PROACTIVE in their financial decisions. This didn't happen overnight, and for the client with the theft problem, it actually took several years to get out of the financial hole he was in. It takes a lot of hard work, focus, perseverance and collaboration between owners and strong financial advisors to review all aspects of their business for efficiencies and find the right path going forward for them. Having a successful business is more than a numbers game, but having good numbers certainly helps!

Most small business owners have an idea of where they fall on the "making money" spectrum. They know about how much money is in the bank account, they know what they roughly invoice monthly or by job, what they need to make payroll, and what, if anything, they are able to pull out of the business for themselves. Mostly they know that they are working very hard and trying to get a handle on the money by the end of the month, or end of the quarter, or end of the year, to give to their CPAs for annual tax reporting. What they don't know is what the real numbers are or what make up those real numbers. They do not have solid accurate numbers to help them with business decisions, and that will lead them nowhere.

MORE QUESTIONS

Additional questions we would ask would be: What kind of business do you have? Is it seasonal? Is it a type of repeat business? Or is your business more one-time, large jobs? Is it a service business or a product business? Are you using technology effectively? Each business requires different financial, budget and cash flow reporting in order for you to understand the current financial situation of your company and where you want it to go.

Do you have a business plan? Have you *written it down*? Having one in your head doesn't count! Have you made assumptions for your estimated growth and current market? How is your market changing? Can you reconcile the plan you may have with how your business is currently doing? Bankers don't loan on air, they loan on documents.

GOALS AND DETAILS

Remember why you started your business. Maybe it was a passion. Maybe you wanted to make money, or make a difference. Maybe both. Are you still working toward your original goal? Is your business achieving your current financial targets or forecasted growth targets? Did your goals change? Where do you want to go now?

All of these questions should be part of your business check-up. It's how you diagnose where you currently are and then set your goals of where you want to be. It's an absolute necessity to look closely at each part of the business, then set up the business in such a way that moves it along efficiently and profitably in the direction you want. It takes a sharp pencil and focus to do such a deep dive, but in the end your business will be all the stronger for it. The DEVIL is not in the details. The ANSWERS are in the details, but it can be overwhelming if you are doing it for the first time or all on your own. You need to approach your financials in a conscientious and detail-oriented way. This book will give you those guidelines for doing it yourself, or what to look for in those you hire to help you. This book will also support the idea that being proactive is better than being reactive, and with strong books and strong support you will be ahead of the game when it's time to grow your business.

Okay. So now let's get started.

Chapter 2

KNOW WHERE YOUR MONEY IS

WHY MAINTAIN GOOD BOOKS?

You already know that it's important to keep a good set of financial books and you already know the reasons that you should understand your financials. We also already know that for most people this is not a particularly fun job to do, but it's a necessity, not a nicety, and most business owners already know that, too. After all, you are an entrepreneur, far from a bookkeeper, but without a good system in place you can literally get buried in all the paper and feel overwhelmed, like trying to eat an elephant. It could get so bad that the IRS is chasing you, and you could lose your business. We have seen it happen. The most difficult lesson for any entrepreneur to learn is that they should stick to what they're good at. Most want to do everything themselves, but that's not always the most efficient or healthy scenario for your business. One of our most trusted CPAs tells his clients, "In the time you waste trying to do your own bookkeeping, you could make far more money doing what you are good at, pay a bookkeeper and have money left over."

Perhaps the hardest part of bookkeeping or accounting is getting over the psychological barrier most people seem to have about it. Many of us don't like to balance our business checkbooks on a monthly basis, much less keep detailed records of where our money comes from and where it goes in our business. Many of our clients even get to the point where they look at a piece of paper and if it has a number on it, they simply give it to us! The fact of the matter is that you don't need to be a financial guru to start your business; you just need to be comfortable with the basics. Just because you are a terrific contractor or marketing consultant or retail shop owner does not mean that you are good at keeping your books, nor does anyone expect you to be. If you are, then that's great, but if you are not, recognize this and seek assistance.

This chapter starts you on your way to understanding what is involved in accurate recordkeeping. While what this chapter provides is important, and what every business owner should understand, keep in mind that it usually makes better sense to use a professional to handle financial management tasks. We have also added a glossary to this book, so you can understand the basic definitions of the financial terms we are going to throw around as we go along. Please refer to it as you need to and if there are items that are not clear, reach out to us, we would be happy to help.

MAKE US BETTER CONSULTANTS

This chapter also helps you become a better client for us. Your goal as a business person should always be to find the "best and highest" use of each and every person who works for you. While we are happy to have the clients who hand us all of their information to organize and report, they are not always getting the "best and highest" use of our talents. If you are able to start with some basic organizational techniques, you will help us help you. We will be able to work at a higher level of performance, ensuring that you truly get your money's worth. We understand that this can be a challenge for some people, and for some, handing us a box of information will be the best we get. We rise to that challenge all the time. But part of our philosophy at Stellar Support Associates is to educate our clients to understand the numbers as much as possible as well, so that they can gain basic financial insight into their own business without our help all the time. We want our clients to be comfortable with their financials and know that they can find answers in them. We are here to not only report, but to also educate.

A strong recordkeeping system is critical because it's the basis of all business information and allows you to learn and use the language of business to make better business decisions. You will need to understand what an Income Statement is, what a Balance Sheet is, what your cash flow includes and what all these mean to you. Realize that your system is only as good as the information you put into it, so put accurate, correct numbers in it. Numbers don't lie. You see all your information right in front of you in black and white.

What does a tax preparer need at the end of the year to prepare your return? They need a Trial Balance, Income Statement and Balance Sheet, they need to know what makes up your journal entries, they need your bank statements, they need a current aging of accounts receivable and they need to know what tax payments you have made during the year, and that the state and federal liabilities and filings have been met. If you don't know what these things are, get a good bookkeeper. If you don't have a good bookkeeper or a good bookkeeping system, you have to come up with this information all on your own and often it gets pushed off and pushed off until April 1st and "scrambling" is not the word for it. Books thrown together like this are not books that give you any sort of information, nor do they allow you any tax or business planning.

One more thing about responsible bookkeeping (we know we said we weren't going to list the reasons it was important, but we can't help it!). Keeping a good set of records on a good software system will help you avoid errors in your tax returns that can subject you to fines and other penalties. If your business is audited, the IRS can make it so much more difficult if your records and books are not in good order. In some cases the IRS may even refuse to recognize legitimate expenses if they are not properly documented. Finally, these financials should also be something that you, as the business owner, can understand to help you make good business decisions – even if you're not a financial wizard. It's YOUR business.

Now sometimes the truth hurts. To actually see the business accurately for what it is might not be pretty at first, but it's certainly necessary. Getting on track with producing this financial information may be painful, but they are good growing pains.

GETTING YOUR ACT TOGETHER

So let's start by getting your act together! Find all your financial information, and get it organized. Here are a couple of exercises to help you with that. We promise that there are only a couple of exercises in this book and the two hairiest ones are right here at the beginning. Let's start with this first one.

EXERCISE:

If you are not using accounting software, pull together and organize by date the following information:

1. Bank statements for each account owned by the business: checking, savings, any credit lines, and get online access. You will also need your check register if you are writing your checks by hand.

2. Credit card statements for all your business accounts, going back as far as you want to track.

3. All the receipts for your business, whether you paid using one of your business bank/credit cards or with non-business/personal account.

Remember, the IRS can request information back many years. In the case of an asset, records related to the asset need to be kept for as long as your business has the asset

PLUS three years. Payroll records should be kept for six years for terminated employees and current employees have no limitations. The IRS can audit returns for the last three years; however, if they feel a substantial error has occurred, they can go back forever. That's a lot of recordkeeping you are responsible for keeping.

Should you use an accounting software system? Fortunately for today's entrepreneurs, inexpensive, easy-to-use software is available that takes financial management tasks and puts them at the tip of your fingers. These wonderful programs, such as QuickBooks, Quicken, Sage and Peachtree have different versions for all different shapes and sizes of businesses and are designed to help even beginners with organizing and reporting their expenses and income. Even if you plan to do all the data entry and financial analysis yourself, an experienced bookkeeper can be invaluable in getting you set up properly and off on the right foot. Furthermore, in order to get the full benefit of these programs, you really need a basic knowledge of accounting in order to run these software packages. *Don't expect the software to do your accounting for you.* Without this basic knowledge, you could get the feeling that you are doing it properly, even if you are not. You shouldn't simply rely on the numbers that your software spits out if you don't fully understand them.

If you have the time and desire to undertake your bookkeeping yourself, there are local classes you can attend to learn how to use these programs and are well worth your time in this case. Lastly, these software programs are so inexpensive and user friendly, it really doesn't make sense to track your finances by hand. Manual systems are usually more time consuming and more prone to errors.

The type of accounting software you use will depend on the amount of accounting knowledge you have. If you don't know what a journal entry, a trial balance, or a double entry is, stick to the more user-friendly versions. Don't get a software system that you need a PhD in accounting to run. It should be easy enough so that if you wish to run a report, you can figure out how to do it. Remember, it's YOUR business.

When should you purchase the program? The short answer is now. Buy it and start to use it as soon as you can. The sooner you put in your data, the sooner you'll be able to get useful information out! Contact an experienced bookkeeper to get you set up and get started.

SET UP YOUR SYSTEM

EXERCISE:

Set up an account for each of your bank accounts and credit cards in your chosen software system and input each transaction. A user-friendly system will help you by setting up a basic chart of accounts that you can start with and add to as need be. After you enter all your information, reconcile it, as you would your personal bank account, and make sure all of your money is accounted for – down to the last cent. If you're not sure if it's a bank, liability, asset or equity account, seek advice. Your Balance Sheet is worthless if these are not correct. We can't tell you the number of times we have taken over an accounting file with each vendor listed as an income account or with checking and credit card accounts never reconciled.

We have a few clients that we call "parachute clients." These are clients that drop in once a year with all their bank statements, check registers, credit card statements and receipts. We enter all their information in Quickbooks, and produce a Profit & Loss Statement and Balance Sheet for the current year for their CPAs. One client actually gives us all of this information in a new Gucci shoebox every year. These business owners know that they would not have the time or patience or ability to pull all this together themselves and they give it to us to do. Depending on the size of the business, it can take quite a few full business days to prepare all this information in the proper manner. While of course we can pull it all together, once a year is NOT enough and this is not the most efficient way to run your business. Just because we are able to produce the information for the CPAs does not mean that these business owners are able to utilize much of the information for analyzing their businesses beyond simple income and expense review. These business owners often see this annual ritual as all they have to do to understand their financials, but this is far from the truth. We don't get an opportunity to work within their financials as the year is going along and make any changes that might be needed to make them more profitable. We don't have the opportunity to set up a budget before the new year starts so that they can set a financial goal for their company and see how they are performing against it as they go along.

Yes, it's true that having a final set of financials after the year is closed is light years ahead of some other small business owners, but the truth is that we are often given this information so late in the tax season and, just like with your CPAs, our client doesn't get their money's worth or "best and highest" use out of what we are able to show them. We cannot stress enough the importance of ongoing bookkeeping services. Recordkeeping should be done regularly. You're doing yourself and your business a disservice by waiting until the last minute and working under pressure. Often times we'll see opportunities that have been missed or expenses that could have been corrected or deadlines that have passed that we could have addressed, had we seen them on time. It takes less time, in the long run, to monitor your finances more frequently; and the potential for those financial benefits definitely outweighs the cost of bookkeeping services.

GIVING ACCESS AND LETTING GO

Who will have access to your records and finances? If you're dealing with an established professional organization, they will have insurance and references and they should have access to whatever information is necessary to perform their job effectively and efficiently. This may mean "letting go" for some people. Your bookkeeper will need access to all your financial accounts. Give it to them. Most will prefer online access so that if something is missing, they can easily download or access the information. Most financial websites will give you the ability to choose the level of access you wish to provide someone, and this level will depend on what tasks your bookkeeper will be performing for you. If you wish for them to pay your bills online, they need to have that access. If you only want them to be able to download statements, that's the level of access you provide. You just want to make sure that they have the ability to perform whatever duties you wish them to do and not be hindered in their execution.

Whether you're working with an outside individual or an employee, you still want to monitor their activity, especially if they have full access. Remember our unfortunate theft example in Chapter 1, it was easy for the office manager because the owner had turned everything over to them and then did not remain active in the financial process. Even if you trust the person, you should review all of your payables and receivables and spot check your bank accounts just to ensure that there are no transfers or payments that you're unaware of.

Get organized and hire an expert. Then make sure that expert produces reports that are clear and that you understand them. Whoever is handling your finances should be able to go through them with you and explain each entry. That's the only way to truly understand your business and make sure you're on the path to success. Your financials are the bricks in that path. Remember, it's YOUR business.

Chapter 3

DOCUMENT, DOCUMENT, DOCUMENT

DOCUMENTING SYSTEMS

Welcome to the most tedious part of bookkeeping and the one that most people dislike so much that they avoid it like the plague. Whether you are a single member LLC, a partnership or a corporation, all entities need to document all of their financial transactions. There are multiple ways of doing this, and it needs to be done. Some people like paper, some like digital. Either way, you need to have your documents in order and kept for upwards of six years, depending on current IRS guidelines. You can't depend on something being available online five years from now. Most banking institutions will only offer 18 months' backup online. For anything further back you would need to make a request (and sometimes pay) for copies and with the wave of banking acquisitions lately you may likely be dealing with a bank that wasn't even your bank to start with.

This documentation process should be very simple and well organized. Once you have used the document to assist in the current year, file it in a place that you can find it again "just in case." Once your system is set up, you don't need to spend too much time or energy on it, but it needs to be done annually.

What, exactly, should you document? The short answer is anything you want to measure: your income, your expenses, what you pay your subcontractors, your vendors and your employees. Yes, that includes pretty much everything, we know, but that's the point. It's important to have the documents to back up all of your business transactions and then it's important to be able to get your hands on that information again when you need it. Let's look at an example of a way to help your business, your tax preparer and yourself.

So let's help your business. Let's say you are a service industry and the hours that you and your staff work are your "work product." If this is your company, then documenting everyone's hours, including your own, is paramount so you can bill your clients correctly. This may sound obvious, but there are many companies or employees of companies who do not do this on a daily or even weekly basis and are always scrambling to bill the client at the end of each month. Sound familiar? Next, there are some small business owners who think they should not keep track of their own hours. They are the owner, after all, and so why be bothered with such a mundane task? Plain and simple: if you need your hours for billing, then of course you do; if you don't need them for billing, then you need them to review your profit margin (a term we will explain fully very shortly). Either way, you need to keep track of them. Make it a habit; keep your hours by client, by day or by task, whichever is most relevant for you.

You will see examples in this book of where we look at your profit margin and we need to know the amount of your time spent for each client or task to see if you made any money. Also, if you have never kept track of your hours as a small business owner, you should, for at least a couple of months. You will see all kinds of trends from this information: how much time you spend in networking and selling, how much time certain clients take, how much time you spend on planning and financials, etc. This information is extremely valuable, especially if you are "always so busy" and "don't have enough hours in the day to get it all done." Being able to answer the questions of where all your time goes is a very handy one. There are many inexpensive or free web-based products that can help, or simply keep a diary or calendar of your activities. This should be something that can be added to your annual retention file for tax purposes – either paper or digital.

So let's help your tax preparer help your business. The best way to explain this is with an example. Let's say that you are a single member LLC with your business out of your home and that at the end of the year you give your CPA a total of auto expenses and the total number of miles you have driven for the year. He or she will probably take a conservative percentage of the total miles driven as a business expense and move on, not wanting to raise a red flag. If, however, you are able to keep track of your ACTUAL miles, even if for just say, three months, he or she can take a much more accurate, and in many instances higher, amount as auto expense.

We had a client who charged all her personal automobile expenses to her business: monthly lease payment, gasoline, repairs and maintenance, license, tax, registration and insurance. Her total automobile expense for the year was $16,000. She estimated that she spent 80% of all the miles she drove as business expenses, but without documentation her tax preparer took a reasonable 25% of the $16,000, or $4,000, as a business expense. The following year, she put a notebook in her car and wrote down her miles every day. It turned out that she drove 20,000 miles per year for her business. With this backup, the tax preparer was able to take 20,000 miles at $.55/mile, or $11,000 as business expenses, thus saving her $7,000, times her tax rate. She now keeps track of her business miles for three or four months every year, just to make sure she is still at her 20,000 miles/year, and adjusts it if necessary.

There are many instances where having the proper backup documents will allow your CPA to take expenses they may otherwise not be able to, so make it a habit. This documentation should also be included in your annual retention file for any possible future uses. One of the easiest forms of documentation is printing out your monthly or weekly calendar to show where you've been and what you do every day. You hopefully will never need this to back up your deductions for a potential audit, but if you do, it could be very difficult to retrieve it years from now.

So now let's help you help your business. The IRS wants receipts, with the appropriate business purpose documented, for all expenses over $40. Keep them! Write on them what they were and who you were with. Attach them to your credit card bills or bank statements, wherever they were charged to. If they are purchases off the internet and you have receipts online, keep them in a specific digital documents file. If you paid for them with cash, keep the receipts and reimburse yourself from your business on a monthly or quarterly basis, to make sure they show up as a business expense. Making sure that each proper business expense is recorded in your financial statements not only gives you the most accurate information to make good financial decisions, it also reduces your tax bill at the end of the year. But don't wait until the end of the year to try and either find or record all of those cash receipts. It's better for your business and for planning purposes to do them at least monthly or quarterly.

A good example of this kind of documentation is when you travel. The big charges – airlines, rental car and hotel – are usually easily documented since you paid for them on your credit card and you usually keep boarding passes, hotel bills and those long green rental car receipts. The tricky part is the smaller items. Often, folks pull cash out of their bank account before they go on a trip to pay for incidentals. A business owner needs to keep documentation of where that money goes, or there will be no good way to document the business expense. Of course, you don't get a receipt for a cash tip for the cab driver or valet or housekeeper, etc. and sometimes snacks or quick coffees or meals are paid with cash. Write it down. Without at least a handwritten note, it is difficult to take any cash transaction as a legitimate business expense. If you gave the cab driver a tip, write it on the receipt. If you gave the maid a tip, write it in your planner. You get the idea. Document what you want to get credit for in some fashion or another so it can be captured and properly reflected in your financials. Many companies have standard expense reports that need to be filled out anytime travel occurs and this allows your bookkeeper to make proper entries and take all relevant expenses. Keeping good notes when you travel is also very important in having the backup you need to withstand the scrutiny of an IRS auditor. Submit your expenses right after a trip. Don't put it off or you'll forget things or, worse yet, you might not get around to it and you'll lose the credit to your business.

FILING SYSTEMS

Organization is everything, and it's the one thing that all good bookkeeping systems have in common. We have seen businesses literally buried in paperwork, like piles and piles of unopened mail and bills, paid and/or unpaid. They know they should hang on to the paper, but not how to control it or file it. A well organized system with accessible, neat files (for both hardcopy and electronic records) not only will keep you on track running your business but will also be a lifesaver during an audit.

Specifically, a good filing system structure allows for you to be able to retrieve business information either by month or by account. A good filing system structure allows for you to be able to encapsulate one full year of documents in one place. Finally, a good filing system structure can be a combination of paper and virtual. The most important thing, though, is to be able to find document backup when you want it.

So what do you need to keep? You need to keep your bank statements along with deposits and cancelled checks. You need to keep three copies of your invoices if you don't have an accounting system: one for the customer, one for the tax preparer and one for you to hold until it's paid. You need to keep supplier invoices to back up your payments to them. And you need copies of your purchase orders if you use them. Lastly, you need to keep all of this with the filings of your tax return for seven years (six plus the current year). This way your retention files can be purged every year so you don't become eaten alive by banker's boxes. The goal is to have all of your documents together by year, and one single year alone, for audit purposes. At the end of each fiscal year, make a backup of anything you have on your computer relating to your business: statements, accounting file, documents, etc. and put it together with any and all documents you may have with your tax return. You do this for two reasons: first, if you are audited by the IRS, you can give them only what they ask for from the year they are asking for it and not ANY other information; and second, at the end of that seventh year, you can take the entire file and destroy it altogether.

There are lots of different filing systems you could have set up. Every person's brain works differently and some people are quite passionate about their systems and how it makes sense to them. Here are two filing systems that have worked best for our clients over the years. You could choose one of these, a hybrid of these two, or design something totally different. The type of system isn't as important as having one.

FILE SYSTEM #1

The first way is to keep all statements, expenses, bills and invoices for a particular month together within a single fiscal year. Start by setting up hanging folders with a tab for each month. As the bank statements, credit card statements, merchant statements, etc. are received, reconcile them in your accounting system and then file them together in the month they cover. You can also add some of your other monthly billings, such as rent, utilities, insurance and other recurring charges to these same monthly hanging folders. At the end of the year, you will have 12 hanging folders and each will encapsulate that particular month. So if you need to find a receipt or a copy of a check for example, you go into your accounting system, find out what the date was of the item you are looking for and then go to that month's folder to find it.

We suggest you handle vendor files differently. Each vendor, especially the larger ones, should have their own file separate from the monthly files. They need separate files because it's easier to follow the flow of transactions that way. Most companies deal with many of the same vendors all the time. You buy inventory or supplies on a regular basis from these vendors all year long, so these vendors should have their own separate file, and not necessarily on a monthly expenses, to make it easier to follow their history of payments. This way, if questions ever arise, and they do arise, you are able to grab the entire vendor file and see the purchase and payment timeline. Sometimes there are returns and credits that need to be kept together or perhaps your vendor is wondering if his invoice from two or three months ago was paid (he was NOT using a good filing system and this happens a lot when vendors figure out your system is efficient). In these instances it's important to keep separate files for vendors within the fiscal year.

Client files and employee files also need to be kept separately from the monthly filing. Client files and employee files can cover more than one year. They usually stay active until the job is complete or the employee no longer works with you. Furthermore, client files and employee files can also contain personal or confidential information, such as credit card information or performance appraisals. You should take care to safeguard these files to the extent of the information they contain.

FILE SYSTEM #2

The second system is just slightly different. Instead of keeping all the monthly bank and credit card and line of credit and merchant banking and utilities statements together by month, you can keep them filed individually by type: a file for each bank account, one for each credit card statement, one for the merchant account statements, and so on. Each utility can have its own file, for example, or they can all be grouped together under one "utilities" file if you don't have that many. That way all of the same types of reports are kept together instead of by month. The difference between this system and the first one really depends on what you feel most comfortable with and how your brain is wired, the organization works either way.

We do suggest, however, that no matter which system you choose for your basic monthly documents, the filing system for your individual vendors, clients and employees remains the same as in the first system.

FILING NOTES

If you want to be paperless, download and file your statements on to your computer and then scan all the receipts. Your filing system should be structured the best way for you to find things as a paper file and then have the ability to retrieve them. If you are using paper and you find a particular file getting too document heavy, it might be a sign that the file should be broken down into smaller pieces. Make sure you have enough physical room in your file cabinet (or whatever you choose to keep the documents in) so that the files don't get mashed in there and it becomes too stuffed full to make it easy to move the paper around.

Remember that the goals for both of these filing systems is to first make sure that you can get your hands on the information you want, when you want it, and second, that you keep an entire fiscal year together so that filing, and then subsequent destroying, can be done easily. All of this centers on the practice of having a filing system, so find what fits you best and start to use one!

RECEIPTS

So what do you do with all those pesky receipts? For the receipts you have that were charged on your company debit or credit card, once again it depends on what kind of filing system makes the most sense for you. School of thought #1 says that you could file them with (or staple them to) the credit card statement they were charged to and put a little check mark on the statement showing that you have the receipt in case you need to find it later.

School of thought #2 says that after you put your check mark on the credit card or bank statement it was charged to, you would then file the receipt into its proper category folder (e.g. meals & entertainment, automobile, computer expense). Whichever of these two ways works for you is fine, as long as you can get your hands on it again if you need to.

CASH RECEIPTS

What do you do if you pay cash for an expense? You still need to have the paper receipt of the charge, and as long as you have that, it's pretty simple. If it's just a single, one-off payment, you enter it into your bookkeeping system by means of a general journal entry to show the expense toward the business. Or if you have several expenses to enter at once, you could fill out an expense report and prepare the general journal entry from that. Either way, you need to determine how you are going to get paid back. You can receive a credit in the books for your paying the expense yourself, or better yet for bookkeeping purposes, the company can issue you a reimbursement check.

What if you use your personal card for a business expense or your business card for a personal expense, by accident? We want to stress that you should avoid doing this as much as possible, because it is important to keep that separation of personal and business at all times. If, however, you have made this error, you can enter it into the system the same way as a cash purchase.

As a business owner, you should take a moment and determine if it's worthwhile for you to have expense reports for you and your employees. If there are very few instances where reimbursements need to take place, then a simple receipt for reimbursement is acceptable. If, however, you and/or your employees need refunds often, implementing a company expense report along with requirements for how large or how often they can be filed will help eliminate unnecessary paperwork for your office manager or bookkeeper. For example, you could say that employees should hold their reimbursements for the end of the month or over $50, whichever comes first.

For heaven's sake, why are we doing all of this?

You're doing all of this because you don't want to ever get a phone call, a letter or a visit from the IRS, your local state department of revenue or a federal marshal and not have all your ducks in a row. One of our clients received such a call and, luckily, all our ducks were present and accounted for and our client was able to testify adequately to a Grand Jury to a positive outcome. Not everyone can say that, and just understand that having complete accurate records could be the difference between a big fine, a potential jail sentence or a refund. Sometimes, federal requests are not even anything that relates to you or your company, but could relate to someone you've done business with and somehow your company name is identified. You never know when good recordkeeping will come in handy so, like a good Girl or Boy Scout, always be prepared.

OTHER DOCUMENTS TO PROTECT AND MAINTAIN

Are your business licenses up to date and displayed, if necessary? Do you have a tickler file or automated file to remind you when to renew with the proper government agency to keep them up to date and in good order? Do you need to provide copies of insurance policies to your landlord or the Department of Labor and do you have a good system that keeps track of when those updates need to occur? Does your business own trademarks or patents? Are the filings for these up to date and do you have a system of keeping track when you need to renew those so they don't lapse? These items can be crucial to a business and should be monitored somewhere. Without good documentation or good follow up, these items could easily fall through the cracks and then leave you scrambling to obtain or update them. Again, a good documentation system is the key.

ONE FINAL WORD ON DOCUMENTATION

Lastly, of course, no filing chapter would be complete without a quick but vitally important discussion about backing up and saving. You hear stories all the time about computers, phones or systems crashing and you need to protect your business from these kinds of disruptions. These days it is very easy and inexpensive to have safe offsite or cloud-based backup systems. Along with automatic backups and flash drives you can easily put in a system of protection, if you haven't already. Your IT person can help you with what works best for you and how to manage the proper levels of password protection. We will further discuss how an IT person should be part of a business team in Chapter 9.

Chapter 4

A MEANINGFUL SET OF FINANCIAL STATEMENTS

BEHIND THE NUMBERS

Different types of companies look at different types of financial statements. These statements, whichever you review for your company, tell you how your company is doing financially over a period of time and/or at a particular point in time. The two most utilized statements are the Profit & Loss Statement (also known as your Income Statement) and the Balance Sheet. We will review these statements ahead as well as several other ones so you can determine which statements you need and what information is most important to the success and longevity of your business. Let's start by sharing the benefits of a well maintained set of financial statements.

1. Failing to keep track of your business's income and expenses is the surest way to endanger your business. Without properly recording and documenting your business, your business is not a business at all, it's a hobby, and no one will recognize it as more than that.

2. Knowing the profit margins and the costs of everything you sell will enable you to price your goods and services properly and make adjustments as necessary. You will significantly improve your odds of making a profit.

3. Analyzing your expenses will allow you to reduce your costs effectively and strategically.

4. Buy vs. Lease? Add an employee? Invest in a building? "What if" business decisions? You will be able to make smart and meaningful business decisions.

5. You will be able to reduce your taxes and penalties, including any state sales taxes and quarterly income taxes by keeping a strong, accurate set of books.

6. Naturally you will be able to reduce your CPA bill and actually get better service with good, well organized information. Suffice to say here that handing your tax preparer a clean set of organized, easy to understand financial statements will make his or her job so much easier and quicker, that they may CHARGE YOU LESS, and they are happy to do so. Often, too, if they receive the statements on a timely basis soon after the year end close (not

April 1st), they are able, as well, to help you with big picture questions and conversations rather than get mired in the details. Your accountant's bill will be less and because you'll get them the information earlier, you will get better attention and information from them. It's a win-win!

7. Are there bank requirements to keep your line of credit? Do you need to have certain amounts of cash in certain accounts or do you need to meet certain accounting ratios in order to satisfy those requirements? Maybe you can only borrow against your current accounts receivable, so your invoicing and collections need to be very current and very accurate. Maintaining accurate current financials will help you report properly and meet these banking requirements without too much headache.

In the past, Bob did not have a current accurate set of financial statements; however, after hiring us this year he did, and this opened up many avenues of savings for Bob. He was truly amazed. First, as the end of the year approached, he was able to see that he would be clearly profitable, so he decided to purchase the new office computers in this year rather than next, so he could write off the expense now, thus reducing his taxable income. Second, because he had a good financial system set up, he could review all of his expenses. He saw that his travel and automobile expenses looked low, and was able to go back and find further legitimate expenses that could be taken by the business. He saw that his advertising expense also looked low and found that the monthly local newspaper bill was being charged to his personal credit card, not his business credit card, so we were able to include that as well. He was able to include his tools and uniforms that he always forgot about now that we were posting all the bank statements monthly. He was able to use these extra expenses to help reduce his income and his tax liability. Bob knew he had missed opportunities in the past to reduce his taxes, and vowed to not do that again.

Finally, and most importantly, in the past Bob often received notices from the state that he was delinquent in his monthly sales tax payments, and was subjected to plenty of penalties and interest over the years. No longer! We are able to record and reconcile Bob's books every month, and Bob makes his monthly sales tax payment for the correct amount and on time, every time. Having proper bookkeeping support to document and control all of his income and expenses accurately allowed him to concentrate on running his business, and doing so with solid accurate financial information.

THE MEAT AND POTATOES OF A FINANCIAL STATEMENT – YOUR PROFIT & LOSS STATEMENT

INCOME

How much a company makes every year is determined by how much income it has less its cost of running the business. There can be a single flow of income, or many different income streams, or even something in between. What is income? Income is all the money you have received for your business's efforts – whether it's for widgets you sell, commission you're paid or fees for services you perform. Income is usually simple to keep track of; it's usually the amount of money made in the form of deposits into your company bank account. If you are paid for your goods and services, report it. It is against the law to not show all the income your business makes in your books, and many folks have been put behind bars for underreporting their income to the IRS. Tax evasion is not worth it, so don't do it.

What do you look for in an Income Statement? You look for a strong trend of increased income and stable or moderately increasing expenses. The income should continue to grow year over year as your business grows, and while your expenses may grow as well, they should grow within an acceptable range with relation to that income. While the income is pretty straightforward, the expenses are usually the things that make the Income Statement tricky. There are those expenses directly related to generating your income, such as the cost of inventory, fixed expenses such as rent and utilities, and variable expenses such as advertising and training. We'll take a look at each in this chapter and start with those costs of goods sold expenses that directly affect the starting profit on everything you do. While looking at income is generally what most people do, determining your profit margin, or how much you make after accounting for direct expenses, is far more important.

PROFIT MARGIN

The best way to explain this concept is through an actual example. The profit margin we are using here is the amount of income you make after all the expenses directly associated with that stream of income (or costs of goods sold) are paid. It's a big picture concept but it is the backbone of every business and determines the health and direction of your company.

Philip owns a marketing firm. His bookkeeping system consisted of locking himself up in his office once a year in January and pulling together all of his "business books" for the past 12 months. After two or sometimes three days of torture, he emerges with what his CPA needs from him. Needless to say, both Philip and his family hated this process, and the information he was gaining was of little use to him because when he embarked on this process, all he wanted to do was get it done as fast as possible. It was very painful and in the end he knew he was making money but not much beyond that. His business was growing and he knew this year he really needed to see exactly how he was doing. Philip certainly needed a business check-up! He hired us over the summer; we took all of his bank statements, credit card statements and vendor invoices and built his financials for the current year in a user-friendly software system, accounting for all the income and expenses for the year to date. This was where the fun started.

Philip had three different sources of income: 1) he taught courses on marketing consisting of workshops and webinars for classes of up to 15 tuition-paying students at a time; 2) he had speaking engagements nationally and internationally; and 3) he had large corporate clients who hired him for both large projects and ongoing contracts. He thought he knew where he made the most income, and of course he was incorrect. After our analysis we were able to determine the following: for Philip's workshops and webinars, while his tuition payments were a good consistent revenue stream, he incurred really high videotaping costs and these workshops required many hours of prep work on his part. For his corporate clients, while they gave him a very strong income by project or monthly retainer, he usually needed to utilize several different subcontractors and this took a big chunk out of his profit. The speaking engagements were the interesting surprise here. While their income was moderate, travel expenses were usually covered or minimal and his presentation was mostly set and he only needed to spend a small amount of time tweaking it for the next audience. Furthermore, and most importantly, he loved being up on stage and would gain many of his webinar students from these speaking engagements.

After having looked at the basic profit margin on each of these incomes streams, we did need to review one last major piece of information. Since Philip's hours were his biggest asset to sell, we needed to see how much time he was spending on each income stream specifically.

Philip had started documenting his hours right after we first spoke, and he was able to also go back several months based on his calendar to get a thumbnail idea of where he was. We were then able to break his work time down into these three different categories to further see where he stood. Philip was correct. The webinars did take many hours to pull together and prepare work plans. Even though he had done several of these by now, the lesson plans continued to need tweaking and he had to spend a lot of time with the students outside of the webinars. The large corporate projects took the next largest chunk of his time and he could see the cyclical pattern of how they hit on certain months of the year, which was a pattern that he did not know existed, and therefore could explore. Lastly, as he had assumed, his speaking engagements required very little prep time and often times the travel to get there took longer than any prep time he needed. These were clearly the biggest money-making opportunities and had the highest profit margin.

Because we were able to utilize his actual data, Philip was astonished to see how each different income stream brought such different profit margins. He was able to make some management decisions quickly with regard to each of those different "products" he sold in order to maximize his profitability while utilizing his time most effectively. We cannot emphasize enough how important a good system of bookkeeping and documentation is in being able to bring such clarity so quickly and concisely. Philip is now able to forecast his future income and how he will get there with the combination of webinars, corporate projects and speaking engagements. He would tell you how awesome this power is!

So, as another example, let's say your business sells the larger one-time project variety "product." You bid for a job, win the job, perform the job. Profit margin is profit margin and the concept is *exactly* the same. What is the income of the job? And what does the job cost you to do? Let's say a contracting company is doing a basic bathroom renovation. Bill, our contractor, has a complete current bookkeeping system in place and has well documented time estimates from his subcontractors and his employees. Bill can tell you how many hours the job will take and how much in total labor cost it will be. He also knows what parts he needs and their costs, and thus knows what mark-up brings him his desired margin. Finally, he knows how many hours of *his* time the job will take and he accounts for that in the bid as well. When Bill bids for a job, he knows what it is going to cost him in parts and labor and what his profit will be. What an advantage he has over his competition. He knows his profit per job and knows how many jobs per year he needs to do to make his desired income. Power to the profit margin!

EXPENSES – WHERE DOES ALL MY MONEY GO?

On a very basic level, there are two types of expenses: those that are fixed and don't change no matter how much you sell and those that are variable, the ones that move with your volume. Most everyone understands these concepts and that's great. In organizing your financials, separate them. This makes it easier to monitor and track. Another way to look at them is that Administration expenses are more fixed expenses such as rent, insurance, utilities and Sales expenses are more variable expenses such as advertising, shipping and training, etc.

EXERCISE:

Start two lists – one with fixed costs and one with variable costs. Side by side is best. List everything on one side that stays roughly the same, month to month or year to year, or rather, how much you spend and can "fix" the cost (within reason). Things like internet service, rent, electricity, health insurance, telephone, auto payment, water, loan payments, etc. On the other side, list things that change with every income source such as inventory, production costs, advertising, travel, supplies, etc. (Payroll is a little tricky. It should probably be added to the fixed side of expenses for this example, but know that changing the amount of current personnel is variable.) Once you know which ones are the same every month and what percentage of your sales they account for, you'll know how much your overhead costs are and can add this percentage to your pricing. Very simply stated (without going into too much detail), divide these expenses by the number of widgets you sell or the number of jobs you do and get an "overhead" cost.

How much should you sell your widget for? You know how much each widget costs you to buy, and now you have a good idea of what your overhead cost is per widget. Add those total costs to the profit you want to make on each widget and this should give you the price you need to charge for each one. We know that we have simplified a very important financial concept here, but if you're not doing this, or some kind of exercise like this, you are not watching your bottom line. If you are not comfortable performing this very important business function, hire someone to help you. Price costing is one of the most important decisions to be made in your business to determine how profitable you will be in business. Make sure you know your costs. Make sure you cover your costs. Make sure you make a profit.

THE BALANCE SHEET

ASSETS

Your assets should equal your liabilities plus your equity. What are your assets? The Balance Sheet lists the assets in order of liquidity, or plainly put, "how close is this asset to cash?" Current assets are the most liquid and include your business checking account and your business savings account and your petty cash, if there is any. Next on the hit parade are your accounts receivable, or who owes you money. This is followed by your inventory, what you have to sell, followed by long-term assets (those farthest from cash status) which can include equipment, furniture and fixtures, or buildings. If you are a photographer, this also includes your cameras. If you are a scientist, this includes your lab equipment, and if you are a contractor, this includes your trucks and heavy tools. Long-term assets are items that need to be counted at the end of the year and depreciated.

LIABILITIES

What are your liabilities? Similarly to current assets, you have current liabilities such as credit cards and accounts payable, and perhaps some vendors who have extended you short-term credit (i.e. 60 or 90 days). Long-term liabilities are things such as loans you made to the business, mortgages on property your business may own or loans on vehicles your business may use.

EQUITY

What is equity? Depending on the type of company you have – an LLC, Partnership or Corporation – on a simple Balance Sheet there are usually three kinds of basic equity accounts: 1) opening balances of any accounts the business starts with; 2) Owner Draw/Investment Accounts show what money you are taking out of the business or having to invest in the business; and 3) Shareholders' Equity or Retained Earnings, or what the business has made since it started (or at least started on your current software!).

What do you look for in a Balance Sheet? In a Balance Sheet you are looking for strong assets of all kinds, substantial checking and savings account balances earning interest, if possible. You are looking for lower receivables which are current, not way past their due dates. You want inventory that is reasonable for the current sales needs and you want the correct amount of furniture, fixtures and computers needed in your company, properly depreciated. For liabilities, usually the fewer you have, the better your company looks. Manageable credit card balances, manageable accounts payable, loans for cars or mortgages for your building with appropriate interest rates are also on there and can give you good information. Lastly, a good retained earnings/shareholder equity is usually a good sign of solid growth for a business and helps with determining the value of the business.

Seasonal businesses have a challenge all of their own. We have a client whose business is basically condensed within four months of the year. Orders start rolling in in late August and early September, product starts being delivered mid-September and the entire season is over by mid-December. The other nine months of the year are spent on planning, ordering, pricing and budgeting. During these four months, funds are put aside to cover the expenses for the rest of the year. It's a budgeting challenge, but this is what keeps the company solvent all year long. Seasonal businesses need to have good forecasts and budgets in order to make sure they don't take too much out of the business in the "fat" months to get them through the "lean" months. It can be very tempting to over compensate, but then you have a problem in the months that do not have a source of income.

OTHER REPORTING

Besides the basic Profit & Loss Statement and Balance Sheet, there are many other reports owners may review on a weekly or monthly basis. Examples of three other popular reports are: a projected cash flow statement, an accounts payable report and an aging of accounts receivable. A projected cash flow statement can be very useful for a company trying to maintain a balance between their payables and receivables. Your accounts payable report tells an owner which vendors are owed and when their payments are due. An aging of accounts receivable report can show an owner who owes the company money and how old those receivables are. There are open invoice reports, payable reports, depreciation reports, etc., and the list goes on and on. If all of the business transactions are entered into the accounting software correctly, there is no end to the amount of financial data an owner can look at and what to measure.

Financial statements can tell so much about a company. More importantly, they can be used to monitor or measure anything you want them to, and many industries have ratios that you can measure yourself against, provided you have the correct information to do so. We don't mean to turn you into accountants with these chapters, we are only showing you the power of this kind of good solid information and what to look for yourself or ask your bookkeeper for.

Chapter 5

SHOW ME THE MONEY

BILLING YOUR CLIENTS

It is essential that you bill for your project or service accurately and on time! Sounds simple enough, doesn't it? Your business income depends on it. Your cash flow depends on it. You need it to pay your staff and your other bills. Yet, often times many of our clients find billing to be the most painful thing they do.

Billing starts with the contract or agreement you have with your client. The contract should include, at minimum, the scope, deliverables with dates, and payment terms. There are many examples of client contracts on the internet, even ones in your line of business, we promise. Some clients use these templates to write their own, or for more complicated, detailed contracts, some clients may seek advice from their attorney. Either way, the important thing to do is to have a contract. Whether you bill periodically based on performance goals or after a certain passage of time, or monthly based on the hours you worked, you know when you have to bill and when you need to bill. Let's take a look at a couple of model companies' billing practices.

BILLING BASED ON A PROJECT

Tom's company installs home alarm systems, either during the new construction of a home or as part of a renovation. He makes a bid on the project, it gets accepted and the client signs the contract. Within that contract, of course, is the scope of work Tom's company will perform along with all accorded details, and the payment schedule. Tom asks for a deposit at the time the contract is signed, a payment when the equipment is ordered and the final amount is due upon completion. He then turns his signed contract over to his office manager along with the deposit check and she enters the new client into the system and deposits their payment. What she does next is to enter the estimated timeline for when she needs to ask for the equipment payment and final payment upon completion.

Having the office manager set up the payments this way does two very important things. First, it makes sure that the payments are invoiced and collected in a timely manner. This makes monitoring the company's cash flow much easier and more accurate. Second, she is able to ensure that the company is never paying out its own money when it's time to order a client's equipment, and the equipment is paid for and on site when they need it. Tom holds a weekly meeting with his, office manager, project manager and CFO to review job status. A week before Tom's company schedules a final "walk through" the office manager sends the final invoice to the client, so that the client has the final payment ready at that time. If there are punch list items at the end which may not be completed due to a construction issue, and this does happen in the world of construction, the final invoice is adjusted to total the work that was completed, with the remaining items "on hold" until they are completed.

The key to Tom's system is that his company is always on top of the billing and collection within the framework of the contract. His staff is active in the project management along the way and Tom and his office manager are constantly analyzing when the payments are due in and monitoring their cash flow.

BILLING BASED ON MONTHLY SERVICE AND PROJECT COMPLETION

Keith runs a brand management and website design company and often has 10 or more projects going on at once. He has contracts with each of his clients as well, but unlike Tom's project-based contract, Keith's monthly billing is tied more to the hours that each associate or project manager or developer works for each client and his clients' payments are much more volatile. His entire staff use an online time management system and each project is set up individually. Each employee posts their hours (ideally) daily, and his office manager checks each Monday morning to make sure everyone's prior week hours are in.

At the beginning of each month, the office manager downloads the required reports from the time management system and produces each client's monthly invoice. The billings are then approved by each project manager, to ensure accuracy as well as to make sure that the project is within its budgeted hours, and the office manager sends them out. Terms for payment are 30 days with a 1% late fee afterwards. These terms are very important for Keith's company, because if a client falls behind on their payments, Keith is quickly able to shift his employees' time to other current clients, until the first client has caught up, therefore not getting "too deep" in labor to any one client. One last item of note, Keith's company also does not turn over the final product until the final payment is made.

BILLING BASED ON MONTHLY FLAT FEE

Margaret has a public relations company. Her contracts contain a full scope of work for a monthly retainer as well as a monthly administration fee. Her monthly PR retainer is collected in advance and her monthly administration fee and expenses are collected in arrears. This means that when she gets a signed contract, it is accompanied by a check for the first month's fee and her staff start working on the client right away. The bookkeeper then adds the client to the system and immediately generates an invoice for the next month's advance fee. Each month after that the bookkeeper issues two invoices for each company: the monthly PR retainer for the next month and the monthly administration fee and expenses for the month just ended. Just like with Keith's business example above, terms are also 30 days with a 1% late fee, and because Margaret's company has this strong billing system, she is quick to see if a client is behind on their payments and can make adjustments to her staff's hours as well. Also, with these billing terms cash flow is consistent and dependable.

WHEN BILLING GOES AWRY

Robert owns a lawn care company and most of the clients he services weekly and bills monthly, or at least he tries to. Robert was working all the time, but didn't have any cash in the bank and could barely pay his bills. We could quickly see a couple of simple things Robert was not doing that could help him right off the bat. First of all, Robert did not have any written contract with his customers. This hurts him in two very critical ways. First, he had no commitment from his clients that they will remain his clients for the course of the season. Second, he receives no protection in case a client decides not to pay after several weeks or even months of service have been received. The next thing we saw, and the reason he called us, was that Robert is also a do-it-yourself type and figures he can do the billing on his own, but often doesn't find the time. What's more is that his clients have given him their credit card to charge, but he just hasn't gotten around to setting them up (yes, he didn't even have to send them a bill, he just needed to charge their card and still couldn't get that set up). Lastly, we saw that organizational skills were not Robert's strong suit, but he just doesn't think he can afford to pay someone to help him with this.

Convincing Robert to hire someone to help him bill was not an easy task at first, but once we showed him what he was leaving on the table he started to see the light. We explained to Robert that he needed to have contracts with his clients for his protection and that he didn't have the cash to pay someone because he wasn't billing accurately or on time. We explained that the cost to hire someone to aid him in having good contracts at the ready and then setting up the billing collections properly for him could easily pay for itself and much more. Robert now knows immediately when someone's credit card expired or was suspended, and so he is no longer working for free!

Steady receivables are always preferable, but some businesses don't lend themselves to this model. If you do have repeat receivables that happen every month, such as a maintenance fee for an association or a membership fee as in a gym, automate the invoicing and billing system. Have invoices automatically sent on a monthly basis or have client credit cards billed automatically on a specific day of the month. This will level your cash flow each month and, in the case of auto-charging a credit card, will ensure the funds are there when you need to pay your bills. The billing can be automated to send emails or paper invoices through most software systems and auto-charging a credit card can be set up with your payment processing company. This greatly improves your collection cycle and cash flow.

COLLECTING THOSE RECEIVABLES

Everyone has experienced slow pay or even "no pay" clients in their business lives. In order to minimize these occurrences, there are several steps you can take. The first is to get a retainer. This may not be normal business practice for some industries, but if yours is one of them, then do it! Collecting partial payment upfront shows commitment for both parties and often weeds out those clients who could potentially not pay.

Next, keep on top of your collections. When you send out your billings, review them often and make sure the clients are reminded prior to when the bill is due. Often just reminding the clients that payments are due keeps them from falling behind, and you can see quickly if there are going to be payment issues sooner rather than later, and that's always the key.

We don't know of any business owner who likes making collection calls. However, if you're the owner and you're the one who's sold the business and working with the client, have someone else make the initial collection call or calls. It takes the "bad guy" image off you and puts it on to someone else at first. For some business owners, it's difficult to work with a client and hopefully sell more to them while asking them for past due money at the same time. Having a bookkeeper or office manager make that collection call removes the stigma from you and makes it "company policy."

Establish a follow-up policy for your business and put it in writing! For example, if the invoice is due in 30 days, set up an email at 25 days, for example, as a reminder, then again at 30 days. Then perhaps follow up with a call and reissued bill from accounts receivable at one week past due, then escalated to finance director after two weeks, then company owner after three weeks. You can adjust this scenario to fit your company.

The most important thing to remember in collections is to make sure you haven't overextended yourself with regard to this client and that if you have to let the client go, you are able to do so without losing too much in revenue. We cannot stress enough that reviewing your receivables often will help you reduce your losses.

What if someone is not responding and not paying? You have several options, depending on the circumstances. You can write off the debt as part of goodwill for the customer and just note this in your customer's file. Should you do business with this person again, you'll know what transpired in the past, and perhaps you can adjust your billings to incorporate the lost income from this current invoice.

If you need to use a collection agency, they are not all created equal, so get a referral. Having outside help also provides some distance from you, as the owner, in collecting the debt, and while collection agencies usually take a percentage, it's always better than getting nothing.

Small claims courts are also an option. You will need to check with your local courthouses to determine the limits of the claims and what paperwork needs to be filled out and filed properly. It's usually an option of last resort, but it has proven successful for many business owners.

PAYING YOUR BILLS

Your company will have several types of bills to pay, and with each type there are different ways to pay them.

PAYROLL EMPLOYEES

Payroll is usually a small business's largest expense. Payroll can be done weekly, biweekly, monthly or quarterly, depending on local state requirements. You can use an outside payroll company to run your payroll or you can run it in-house, depending on how many employees you have and how complicated (i.e. health insurance, other benefits, 401k) it is. Whether you use an outside company, or do it in-house, your payroll people need to keep current all of the reporting depository requirements. Without proper expertise, your business can get into a whole bunch of trouble really quickly if proper payroll processing does not take place. We discuss this further in Chapter 8.

INDEPENDENT CONTRACTORS

Subcontractors are a very effective way to help supplement your staff. While the cost per hour may be higher than what you pay a permanent employee per hour, because you aren't paying benefits and overtime, etc., the ultimate cost to your company may be much less and could provide your company with the specific support necessary at a particular moment in time for a specific need. Yes, subcontractors are vital to many small companies, but you need to ensure that the subcontractor is truly an independent contractor, according to the IRS. The IRS states: "If you are a business owner hiring or contracting with other individuals to provide services, you must determine whether the individuals providing services are employees or independent contractors." Questions you need to ask in determining whether or not they are subcontractors are:

1. *Behavioral:* Does the company control or have the right to control what the worker does and how and when the worker does his or her job?

2. *Financial:* Are the business aspects of the worker's job controlled by the payer? (these include things like how the worker is paid, whether expenses are

reimbursed, who provides tools/supplies, etc.).

3. *Type of Relationship:* Are there written contracts with each subcontractor or are they offered employee type benefits (i.e. pension plan, insurance, vacation pay, etc.)? Will the relationship continue and is the work performed a key aspect of the business?

Businesses must weigh all these factors when determining whether a worker is an employee or independent contractor. Some factors may indicate that the worker is an employee, while other factors indicate that the worker is an independent contractor. There is no magic or set number of factors that makes the worker an employee or an independent contractor, and no one factor stands alone in making this determination. Also, factors which are relevant in one situation may not be relevant in another. The key is to look at the entire relationship, consider the degree to which your company directly controls the work the subcontractor does and to document each of the factors used in coming up with the determination. If the subcontractor is working for other companies besides yours and is actively soliciting other companies to work with, there's a pretty good shot they are an independent contractor. If you are the only client this person has and they have a desk at your place and business cards from your company, they are most likely considered an employee and should be on the company payroll. If you are still unsure, ask your accountant, because each state has different standards.

INVENTORY

Your next largest expense could be inventory, especially if you are a wholesaler or run a retail company. Where payroll is something you can't really establish payment terms for, financing inventory is negotiable. Ask your vendors for payment terms that cover 30, 45 or 60 days. If your vendors offer 2% 15, net 30 terms (meaning that the bill is due in 30 days OR if you pay the bill within 15 days, you can have a 2% discount) and you have the cash flow, pay it in 15 days if you can and take the 2%. Further, some vendors offer 60 day payment terms and if this is appropriate for your business, take advantage of these terms. Ask your vendors for rebates once you hit a certain purchase level. Sometimes you can save money by ordering larger quantities in order to hit rebate levels or large order discounts. This can be especially helpful on items that you use over and over again. Shipping can easily add 2 – 5% to your inventory costs. See how you can group orders together in order to minimize these shipping costs whenever possible and/or review your shipping costs, especially for your larger vendors, and ask them for more favorable shipping rates. And ask your vendors for reduced, or better yet, free shipping, based on your purchasing history.

Seeking terms or other reductions in inventory payment should always be a priority for your business, if it relates to you. This also helps tremendously with your cash flow situation. By seeking and receiving terms on your inventory, you can have the inventory working for you (i.e., turn it into profit for you) before you have to pay for it. Also remember to check your invoices, if you are a reseller, to ensure that you are not paying sales tax since you bill your customer sales tax. Notify your vendors that you are tax exempt and provide them with your tax certificate. It's a very simple task, but one that could save you and your customer some money if you are reselling the product. Remember most vendors would rather negotiate with a current customer for better terms or shipping costs than have to go looking for new customers. Ideally, it's to your advantage to have more than one supplier for what you need, but if that's not possible, remain vigilant with regard to your inventory costs and review them often.

So how do you protect your inventory? Well, first you count it. You count it at the end of the year at the minimum, and more often if possible. If it's too large to count all of it on a monthly basis, let's say, then you spot check it to your accounting inventory log periodically. Second, you lock it up to keep it from walking away. Make one person in charge of the inventory from when it comes in to when it goes out. It needs to be under one reliable person's care. Inventory shrinkage is a large cost to businesses.

Is all your money tied up in your inventory?

Inventory is a tricky thing and a company can quickly become inventory heavy and cash strapped. Managing the amount of inventory needed is an art as well as a science and needs to be watched closely. Too little and you could lose business, too much and you might not have the cash to pay your bills. Many industries have mathematical ratios or inventory turns that will keep your business in line and your financial health strong. It is important to seek out this information and utilize it in concurrence with what you know about your jobs and your market.

We had a client very successful in selling high-end decorative accessories and she was coasting along in her success. When the economy was booming, inventory flew off the shelves to locations such as Neiman Marcus, Bloomingdales and other high-end stores. When the economy declined in 2008, her sales also slumped and the demand for these items dropped like a rock. She wasn't paying as close attention as she should have been. The company was having products produced in China so the lead time from production to inventory to sale was over a year. The financial crash was quick and when so many orders were cancelled from buyers, production was already in process and could not be cancelled. The warehouse was overflowing with merchandise, the company's Balance Sheet was lopsided; no income was forthcoming. This was one of those times when difficult decisions needed to be made and a business owner needed honest and trustworthy advice. She sold as much of the inventory as possible to previous buyers and wound up selling a large portion of the inventory to discount stores, such as Home Goods and BJ's. While no one could have predicted the depth of the economic troubles of that period, business owners need to be vigilant in monitoring their inventory exposure.

OTHER PAYABLES

Other monthly expenses such as credit cards, utilities, office expenses, rent, car payments, business loan repayments, etc., need to be reviewed and paid on a timely basis and utilizing a solid cash flow forecast is a good way to do that. It can be as simple as laying out each month by date when all of your bills are due vs. your cash flow. This way you can see forecasted trends of which weeks are going to be tighter than others and you can plan accordingly. It is important to review all of your bills on a regular basis. There is usually some room for reduction in electricity rates, cell phone contracts, etc., so keep a close eye to make sure you are not paying too much.

Some special words about company credit cards, they are another place to negotiate. Seek lower interest rates on the card or cards you currently use or only take the cards that offer you competitive rates. Seek miles or cash back or other rewards for using your card. And seek the proper credit limit for your business. With so many credit card options to choose from these days, you can find the right credit card to handle how you run your business. One word of warning though, credit card rates, even when negotiated down, are still higher than just about any other cost of debt. If you have to run a balance on your credit card from one month to the next, you should make sure you have exhausted all other avenues of borrowing.

A WORD ABOUT ASSETS

A discussion about showing me the money would not be complete without a conversation about the rest of your company's assets. Your most current assets are your checking and savings accounts. Contacting your bank periodically to make sure you have the correct type of accounts for your business with the lowest fees possible is just good business practice. Your next most current asset is your accounts receivable, and we have already discussed those. Finally, make sure you review your other assets as some companies have way too much of their true cash buried in them. First let's look at inventory. Once you've negotiated the best payment terms and pricing and shipping rates, take a step back and see if you have the correct amount of inventory you need. Do you have too much? Is too large a portion of your money tied up in your inventory? If relevant, how close are you to having a just-in-time inventory? It's vital that you do a review of your supply to see if you are operating efficiently. Also do you have the right kind of inventory? The most critical thing is to make sure that you use your cash in the best way possible, so making sure your inventory is the correct amount and correct mix needs to be reviewed continuously.

Most furniture, fixtures and equipment assets are usually pretty big and bulky or even permanently attached to your office and don't walk away often. These Balance Sheet items such as desks, copiers, computers, production equipment, etc., are depreciated over a specific period of time on a monthly or annual basis. Some equipment can be listed as an asset of the company, but expensed on your annual Profit & Loss Statement instead of being depreciated over time, and some different types of equipment can be depreciated over different periods of time and may even have depreciation accelerated. What is best for your business can vary depending on the type of business you have and the life expectancy of the equipment. This is a discussion that is best suited for your tax preparer.

It is most important that a business owner both invoice their clients and pay their own vendors on a timely basis. You've heard the saying, "Cash flow is King"; that couldn't be more true. If you are able to manage the flow of money in and out during a month, you will be able to manage the profitability of your business. Next, let's see how to do that.

Chapter 6

BUDGETING AND FORECASTING

HOW DO I MAKE THE MONEY I WANT TO MAKE?

Well run businesses start with a budget and a forecast, and update them annually. Budgets and forecasts of two to three years are usually required for any funding and there is a reason for that. Everyone needs a plan. Your budget is your plan of where you are going for the next 12 months. A budget not only sets up your financial structure, it gives you the place to start. Often it can tell you if you should start this business or not. It tells you what your expenses are going to be based on what you think it will cost you to set up or run your company and therefore give you a basis to measure your progress against. Your forecast is your plan for where you think you are going to go several years down the road. It takes into account assumptions about your income based on market growth, and your expenses based on what you think you'll need to run the business at the level of income you wish to achieve.

If you know that you can't pull these documents together on your own, hire someone to help you. And the more solid your books are, the easier the process will be. You will need to make assumptions for the upcoming years based on your prior year actuals, relevant economic data, relevant marketing data and cost of living adjustment increases. You'll use your "best guesses" based on these assumptions and produce a useful document for where your company is going. Entire books have been written on budgeting and forecasting, so we'll stick to the basics here and look at two very simplified examples of how to produce these reports.

FORECAST WITH NO HISTORY

Roberta needed a business plan for opening a new retail store. She had many years of experience in retail, so she did understand what inventory levels were needed and how much she needed to sell of her own items vs. consignment items in order to hit her income levels. We spent a lot of time together determining what kind of investments she needed to make in a new store fit out, new packaging and collateral, online advertising and staff. What we weren't sure of was what her sales would be when she opened the doors in September, and thus, what level of capital she needed to have on hand. Since we had nothing to compare to, we developed five different scenarios of what her first 18 months could look like. We had her best guess sales budget, one that was 30% higher in sales and 50% higher in sales, and one that was 30% lower in sales and finally 50% lower in sales. Each of these scenarios produced different expenses and different cash needs, so we were able to determine what we needed in reserve in order for her to be properly funded. This turned out to be invaluable in getting the capital she needed lined up before she actually opened the doors.

FINE TUNE YOUR FORECAST

Barbara had gone through the exercises and understood her profit margins and knew which parts of her business were making how much money. She had enough cash to pay all of her bills and make a profit each month. Barbara wanted a certain level of income and wanted to know how to get there. What would it take to get there sales wise? And what were her costs each month? Setting up a budget and forecast for her was the right answer. The best way to start with Barbara was to take her current financial statements and make adjustments and assumptions in order to have her hit her financial goals and then monitor her monthly progress against those goals. We love this part and we like to start at the bottom!

Barbara's consulting business currently made her a net profit of $150,000/year. She wanted to make $250,000 in the next two years and thought a 30% annual increase for this period was possible based on market projections, and was a good goal for her to shoot for. Her business was not seasonal, so a gentle concentrated monthly increase seemed the most possible for her to achieve mathematically. We spread out the income increase evenly by month, taking her original monthly net income of $12,500 and increasing it by 2.5%/month, so that at the end of Year 1 she would be earning the equivalent of $16,250, or

$195,000/year. We then continued this for another year at the same 2.5% rate increase and by the end of Year 2 her monthly income was $21,125 or $253,500/year.

Next we looked at Barbara's expenses individually. We knew in order for her to hit her goal of 30% per year increase in sales, she was going to need to spend more on variable costs, such as advertising and business development, and that she was going to need to hire an additional employee at the end of Year 1. In reviewing her fixed costs, we knew her rent was going to step up $500/month in Year 2, and she was going to have to increase her travel and meals probably by 10% due to increased marketing activities. For the remaining expenses in this example, we made a COLA adjustment of 2% (i.e., office supplies, computer expenses, etc.).

So looking at this simplified example, if we know what the bottom line needs to be for each month and we made solid educated estimates to our expenses, both variable and fixed, for each of those months, we just needed to go back into the total sales number for the month to set up a budget to use going forward. When we were finished, Barbara knew what she had to do and had a plan on how to get there.

YOUR ASSUMPTIONS

It's important to remember several things when putting together an attainable budget for a small business. First, what are the current market conditions and what do you believe them to be in the time period of your budget. Second, this may be a combination of some research on your part and your experience. Either way, look closely at those marketing conditions and your current market and make your best guess assumptions. Third, realize that expenses do move around, so review each of them carefully for what the volatility could be. Your inventory costs move and your service costs change. Advertising and marketing costs will need to be adjusted if that is going to be your push for the following year. Will you need new computers soon? Will you need the help of different types of professionals as well as your current subcontractors or employees? All of these are very volatile and all of these are very important to consider. The better your guesses are for all of the numbers in your budget, the more accurate your budget will be in helping you succeed in hitting your goals.

WORKING WITH THE HIGHLIGHTS

So let's review the highlights of why you are setting up a budget. It's important to set goals for yourself, and set them at different levels if you wish to. Modest increases or stretch goals can all be accounted for in a budget, it's up to you. Understand your market and the current marketing conditions. Often times different industry organizations offer their own assumptions of their business market, and that can be very helpful. Next perform a careful review of all of your expenses, variable and fixed. If the expense is dependent on your sales number, make sure it moves with the increase (or decrease) in sales. Does your inventory reflect your sales increase? Will you be implementing a new marketing strategy? Make sure to account for any additional employees (front line and back office) or independent contractor help you may need, and if those employees or subcontractors will create any additional expenses (i.e. travel miles, company car, and advertising). For your fixed expenses, review them carefully to see if there will be any large foreseeable movements coming down the pike.

Then review your budget along with your monthly financials! Some accounting software out there allows you to input your budgeted numbers directly into the system so you can quickly see where you are falling short and need to pay more attention or where you are overachieving and may need to make more investments. Your budget is your yardstick to measure how well you are doing. Instead of just looking at a monthly financial statement to see how you did, you look at those same monthly financial statements and see where you need to go. It's a shift in how to think about your business – from reactive to proactive financial management.

Chapter 7

HUMAN RESOURCES

ALL SHAPES AND SIZES

We've all heard the saying "An organization is only as good as its people." Some small businesses consist of just the owner; some small businesses consist of an owner and some back office people; and some small businesses consist of an owner, or several, and people who represent the company and the owner to clients outside of the office. Managing your human resources is often managing your most expensive asset and just like any other asset, it needs to be monitored for its cost and its efficiency. Whether you have a group of independent contractors who you call upon as needed or full-time employees with benefits, the managing of your human resources is still basically the same. Maybe your employees need continuing education classes to keep their licenses up. Or maybe you want to offer staff development to your key employees in order for them to be prepared for a promotion within your company.

Your company needs a policies and procedures manual for them to follow in order for you to get consistent, complete and correct help from them.

Now, we hear you all moaning and see all the cringing! Moan and cringe all you want. You know it's true, but business owners often see investment in policies and procedures as the least productive of their time. If you take the time to set them up and implement them, you won't believe the headaches you will save yourself from down the road. Besides, it won't take as much time as you think and often you can get your employees to help with the task. Many employees will find the opportunity to write down everything they do therapeutic, and they too will be able to evaluate what they do and perhaps find some efficiency that can be improved upon. Plus writing down a person's complete job responsibilities can help you as an owner to value their position more accurately and allow for easier comparison if you speak to others in your same industry.

STRUCTURE OF YOUR COMPANY

If you are just starting a business, you have a unique opportunity to set up a structure before the business even opens its doors. You can think about how the organization will look a year from now, two years from now or five years from now. What each position will be responsible for and what the responsibilities and duties are for that position and how it fits within the organization. If your business already exists, you can still do the same exercise but within the structure of what you currently have in place and step back to see if that picture is delivering what you need it to deliver. A company structure gives your employees a clear line of authority and allows you, as the business owner, to alleviate yourself of all of the daily business operations. You would like to be able to take a vacation and still have your business run well while you were gone, wouldn't you? Or be able to retire one day and either sell your business outright or hand it to the next generation, knowing that it can run on its own without your daily input, correct? Now we are not advocating empire building or adding extra layers of "fat." What we are advocating is setting down on paper a company structure that can grow as you grow.

Start from the top. What are the responsibilities of the CEO and who will fill that job? If you are the sole owner of the business, of course it is you; however, let's say you have an LLC with another partner. Which of you is better qualified to fit that post? List the responsibilities, measurable goals and deliverables, the qualifications that person needs to move to the next job. Next jobs to look at are VPs of Marketing, Operations and Finance. Each of these positions requires a different set of talents and responsibilities. As you write down the specific responsibilities of each of these positions, also include how they report up through the organization. Next determine which jobs will be needed under each of these VPs, and so on, until you have gotten down to the most basic employee. After laying this all out on paper, you will have your basic organizational chart and can begin to see what the structure of your business should look like. This is also the basis of how you start to hire people into the different areas of your business. With good solid job descriptions in place, you can fill these jobs with employees who can easily understand what is expected of them and what they need to do to get promoted.

When Lorraine and Michele (that's us!) first decided to combine our two finance businesses together, we actually performed this basic exercise and we were surprised to see how obvious it was as to which of us would start off with which job. We actually did not know who would fill the CEO role at first. We went right to the VP positions: Marketing, Operations and Finance. It was very clear to both of us that Lorraine was happiest when she could manage the office staff and push the work through, thus she would be VP of Operations. We added further responsibilities to Operations such as managing the efficiency and pay of the staff and what types of clients the current staff could best respond to and when they were ready to add new clients and what size they could be. Michele was a natural networker. She liked to go to events, meet new people and knock on doors. Michele was very successful at selling the bookkeeping services and added the additional measureable matrix of the number of new clients to be added per month/quarter/year and the size of those clients to that position. The VP of Sales & Marketing was born.

After listing the job responsibilities of the VP of Finance and CEO it once again became clear that until we were big enough to replace ourselves, Michele would be VP of Finance and Lorraine would be CEO. We went on to fill the organizational chart with all the positions we needed under each of the VP positions, knowing that we had people in place to fill many of those jobs, and it quickly became obvious what positions needed to be filled right now and what jobs needed to be filled down the road. As these middle managerial positions would be filled by our current staff, as they progressed and grew into higher level jobs, Lorraine and Michele's level of responsibilities moved higher and higher up the organizational chart until we had created a company structure that could run on a day-to-day basis without us.

JOB DESCRIPTIONS AND CROSS-TRAINING

Lucy, an experienced retail marketing executive, was just hired by a manufacturing business as VP of Sales. Her new company was in need of an entire revamp of its sales division, as it was time for the company to expand into the next region and it needed a solid proven plan. Lucy started her job on May 10th. On May 25th as she was training for her summer triathlon on her racing bike, a distracted car swerved out of their lane and hit her and her training partner and sent them flying. Lucy was not critically injured, but did find herself in the hospital with broken ribs and a concussion, out of work for several weeks.

Steve was an office manager of a small installation business. He was responsible for all of the accounting and billing and scheduling for his company, one of those folks you just can't do without. His father, retired in Florida, slipped and fell and Steve needed to fly down there for a couple of weeks and arrange his father's recovery and follow-up care.

Robert was the head designer for a large architectural firm in Chicago. He had a great eye for hiring the best new young talent and cultivating them into top designers. He was responsible for a huge amount of the growth in his firm for the last several years. Robert's wife was offered a CEO position in Boston and he was gone 30 days later.

Stuff happens. People get injured, they get sick, they need to take care of loved ones and sometimes they pass away unexpectedly. Folks also go on vacations, maternity leave and get transferred. Some people resign and some get fired. The only sure thing you can say about people is that change is always happening. You, as a business owner, cannot take the stance that everyone will stay in their current positions and never leave you. They *will* leave you, and while it might not be permanent in some cases, they will leave you at the most inconvenient or unexpected time – is there ever really a good time? And then you have to bring in someone new or have a current employee cover for them. While it's a luxury if they are able to learn their new job from the person leaving the job, it doesn't always happen. Often someone new has to come in cold and it's usually you, as the business owner, teaching them what their new job responsibilities are. And who has time for that?

So, in an environment where you know unplanned changes could happen at any moment, what can you do to protect yourself? Your protections are called Procedure Manuals and Cross-Training.

It is imperative to have job descriptions for each employee at your business, so get started by taking these four steps:

Step 1 – If you currently have employees in these positions, start by asking them to document all the different tasks they perform. No task is too small, and have them categorize these tasks by how often they do them (i.e., daily, biweekly, monthly, quarterly, etc.), you get the idea.

Step 2 – After they have written down everything they do, then have them go back and write down how to perform each task in such a manner that if they were not there to perform that task, someone could pick up their directions and follow them. This is lengthy, but it doesn't have to be done all at once. Start with one task each day, writing no more than 10 or 15 minutes each day, and in a couple of weeks you'll have all of the tasks documented.

Step 3 – Have someone else try and follow the steps. Cross-training is not only healthy for your body, it's healthy for your business.

Step 4 – Review Steps 1 through 3 periodically.

What if your employee is new and that position didn't exist before? If you've done the above structure exercise you'll be on your way. Start with a list of job responsibilities for that new hire and let them begin to document how to perform each task as they do them. You'll certainly need the list of job responsibilities anyway in order to hire someone for the position, and if you were able to set up your organization before you actually started, both of you should have a good basis to start from.

What if it's a type of specialty position such as engineer or designer? No different. Besides a general job responsibility such as "design and layout installations of video equipment in residential homes," there will be other more specific job responsibilities that fall within the scope of that job. And yes, you will need to hire another engineer, for example, but then you will already have in place specific tasks your company requires written down.

What if I'm too small and don't have anyone to cross-train? You, as the owner, may be the person to fill that job until a replacement is found, so make extra sure the job tasks and directions are easy to follow.

And my favorite question: What if we are so busy that we don't have the time to stop and write this all down? Think about the alternative. Now just do it. Remember proactive, not reactive.

HUMAN RESOURCE POLICIES

Human resource policies can be a little tricky. Sometimes less is more and sometimes more is more. If you are a smaller company, you may not want to put too many policies in writing to allow for maximum flexibility, especially with the smaller number of staff. If you are a larger company, you generally need more policies so that all of your employees are treated equally. You will need to find your match of size vs. policies and you will need to implement them. More and more these days even smaller companies are being required to have written policies, i.e. handbooks, as the workforce continues to develop. Make sure you check the federal and/or state regulations for your industry to be in compliance. Having said that, let's look at some general areas to cover. Yes, we know it is more documentation, but it too is necessary.

Vacation – What is your vacation policy? Is it different for different types of employees? Do your "years of service" come into play in the equation? Do you require vacations to be sequential (two weeks all together, like banks still do) or can they be taken at the employee's discretion?

Sick Days – How many sick days do you allow an employee before they need to "pay" for them with their vacation or not be paid for them at all?

Note: Make sure you accrue vacation and sick days on a monthly basis. For example, if an employee is entitled to 10 vacation days per year, they accrue, or earn, .8 of a day each month instead of getting it all up front at the beginning of the year. Same thing for sick days. This way, if they leave in the middle of the year, you only pay for the vacation and sick days they have earned.

Corporate Holidays – Does your company offer certain holidays off for everyone? What are they? Do you have them on a corporate calendar? Are these above and beyond an employee's vacation?

Note – As your organization grows, it's good to have an overall company calendar where someone in the company knows where all the staff are at all times. This calendar combines company holidays, employee vacations, and employee appointments. This job responsibility usually falls under the office manager's duties in one form or another. It may also be monitored by the person answering the phones. It is vital to know where everyone is or how they can be reached during the day. Also it is good to have not just regular contact information on everyone, but also some additional contact information in case of emergencies. This information should be held in a secured place by a manager.

Maternity Leave – Not just for girls anymore! What are your state statutes? If your business is too small to require the state statute to kick in, what do you want to extend to all of your employees?

Benefits – Will you offer medical or dental coverage? Will you offer a 401k? Profit sharing? Matching 401k? How long will the employee need to be working for you in order to take advantage of these benefits? If it's appropriate in your industry, or even if it isn't, use your benefits package to attract and retain good talent.

Termination – Make sure that when you terminate an employee you follow all the state guidelines and have proper documentation of the reason for termination. If it is for cause, document it in their personnel file. If it is for lack of work, document that also. You never know when you may need to refer to this and you don't want to leave it to memory. That is not proper documentation.

Discrimination Clauses – In today's environment, it is imperative that you express your company's beliefs and that they are appropriate with any regulations. Your company's stance on racial, sexual orientation or age discrimination all need to be reviewed and determined.

Confidentiality and Non-Compete Clauses – These are very good things to have in any employment documentation, and of course it is more important to certain types of jobs within an organization than to others. It is also important to consult legal counsel or a qualified HR consultant when putting them together, depending on how important or proprietary your company information is.

Our Big Fat Disclaimer – This is NOT an inclusive list of policy topics and you may have additional specific topics that need to be addressed. Your company may require drug and alcohol testing for employees, instruction on how to operate machinery, or rules on how to drive company vehicles. Consulting a list of your industry practices is a good place to start.

And these policies are what you use to draw up your employment contracts. A good employment contract has several different elements in it, so let's take a look.

EMPLOYMENT CONTRACTS

1. Specific Job Responsibilities and Measurable Goals. As we discussed earlier in this chapter, listing out the employee's responsibilities eliminates discussion and miscommunication later, as does listing the goals and expectations that the employee will be held to as his performance is reviewed. The most important thing here is to have specific job responsibilities along with clear measurable goals for the employee to attain.

2. Salary/Pay – How much and how often? Hourly or salary? Any additional commission or bonuses?

3. Review Process – When will your employee receive a performance review? Is this when raises are discussed? Make it clear that this is where their performance vs. expectations will be reviewed.

Note: This review process is of special importance when it comes to releasing an employee. If you are able to document events and discussion dates and times with an employee, you have a better case for when you need to let an employee go for cause. You can, of course, have reviews more often if necessary, and this can only strengthen a case.

4. Your list of specific company policies listed above.

5. Company Core Values and Principles – how they represent the company and themselves? What is expected of them when they are interacting with a client or vendor? Remember, they are representing your company and, therefore, an extension of you.

Sunshine Company had quickly grown to nine employees over 18 months. When we got there to run their bookkeeping, their employee files were not really files, but more like one big pile of goo. We couldn't tell if we had the required information for each employee, i.e. basic info sheet, tax forms, I-9 forms, etc., because there was not a file on each individual employee. While they did have signed employee agreements for each employee, each agreement was different in the area of which HR policies it covered.

It turns out that the three owners were using three different types of agreements, and depending on which of them had the time to write up the agreement, that's whose agreement was used. Some agreements touched on certain policies and other agreements touched on others. Also it didn't occur to any of them that they could accrue vacations and sick days monthly, so when their last employee left in April, he was able to get the full year's worth of vacation days even though he had only worked barely four months! Of the two project managers they had, one of their agreements listed specific job responsibilities and measurable duties, and the other did not. Luckily, within the wording of each agreement it was stated that the agreements could be changed at any time. We worked closely with the partners to draw up one agreement with policies that worked consistently across the board and put those files together gathering all the missing information.

In wrapping up our discussion of job descriptions, procedures and policies and employment contracts, just know that there are many online resources and "do it yourself" websites that you can use. You can sec examples of company policies and employment agreements and develop your own from there. Furthermore, you need to learn about and consider state and federal guidelines regarding any of these topics to ensure you are covered as it relates to your industry. Lastly, it is a lot of information and there can be exposure for you, so taking advantage of an attorney or HR specialist might be a good investment, so that you are covered and perhaps have considered everything specific to your industry.

PAYROLL COMPANIES

Brian's company used a local payroll company to run his bi-monthly payroll. This company processed all of his employee's payments on time and seemingly correctly and they did so for a good couple of years. All of a sudden he received a letter from the state saying that he was behind in his employee withholding taxes for the last two quarters. It was thousands of dollars and the funds certainly had come out of his bank account like clockwork. He contacted his payroll company to see what the problem was only to find out that the company had declared bankruptcy and closed its doors. Brian was stuck. He was still responsible for those payments to the state, even though the payroll company was supposed to be making the payments. He currently has a suit pending, but there are no assets left in the payroll company, so it does not look good.

If you are going to use an outside payroll company, make sure it's a highly reputable organization and then still check up on them. Payroll is a tricky thing, not only because of the accounting for it, but rather because the laws and withholdings do change, so if you are going to process your own, you need to keep up with these changes in the laws. There are many good payroll companies out there, and they are becoming more and more price competitive all the time.

So let's start with how many times per month you need to run your payroll. Some states regulate this and some do not. Some types of occupations are traditionally paid certain ways and employees will also have those expectations. You will need a review to make sure you are in compliance with regulations. Some companies have everyone on the same payroll cycle and some companies have different cycles for different types of employees, it depends on what you decide.

Now let's look at whether to use an outside agency to run payroll or to run it internally. Cost vs. expertise is usually the deciding factor. Accounting software is sophisticated enough to handle it for you with minimum training on your bookkeeper's part, including automatically making the changes to state or federal withholding or tax rates. If you have the staff to handle it, you may not need to incur an additional cost. If, however, you do not have the staff, nor want to add additional training, you may want to use an outside company. Their costs vary by company and by the type of payroll run you are looking for. Costs are lower if you input your payroll information online. Costs are lower if you input your payroll information on time. Costs are higher if you require paper statements sent to employees and costs are higher for direct deposits. Also make sure you ask not only what the periodic payroll run will cost you, but also what they will charge for quarterly and year end filings. Often companies charge lower payroll run fees to get you to sign up, but then hit you hard for the quarterly and year end reports.

Our best advice is to shop around for a good local payroll representative and stick with them. Know that some payroll companies pay their representative only when they first bring in a new client, not every year the client stays with them, so depending on which payroll company you use, your payroll representative may be more or less responsive than another. Also, most payroll companies will have a representative set up your payroll account then turn you over to an inside payroll specialist. Review their fees periodically and if you have any questions, call your representative right away. Payroll companies are now expanding into other areas such as 401k and insurance and benefit administration, so if you need these types of services, that may also be another reason to use an outside firm.

If your employees are your company's biggest asset, make sure you are protecting your company and protecting them. Guidelines and backup is the best way to do that, so investing in policies and procedures and making sure your structure is set up optimally will all make such a difference in operating your business. Once again, you can go from being a reactive manager to a proactive manager.

Chapter 8

BUILDING YOUR SUPPORT TEAM

IT TAKES A VILLAGE

There are certain support people every business and business owner needs to help make their business successful. You have so many decisions to make on a day-to-day basis in running your business that it's important you are able to sleep at night regarding items outside of your business. It is critical that you have certain professionals to call upon when you need them, and it is important that they are experienced, talented and have unquestionable integrity. Usually the best place to find these professionals is through referrals from other trusted colleagues. For many positions, you are able to check credentials through professional organizations and word of mouth.

BOOKKEEPERS

A bookkeeper's main job is to account for all of the transactions of a company, the assets of the company and the changes in those assets. The bookkeeper is responsible to four different people: 1) the owner, who wants to know what the income is and what the assets look like; 2) investors, who want the same things as the owner, plus they see the bookkeeper as an independent "recorder" of this information; 3) lenders or bankers, who want this information so that they can ensure they can get paid back; and 4) the accountant, who wants this information to ensure that the taxes they are filing for the company are an accurate representation to the various tax entities.

A bookkeeper controls all the source documents that come into the company, from start to finish. They record all of the transactions from those documents and reconcile the associated accounts. They prepare adjusting entries, if necessary, to close the books for each period, and they prepare the financial statements for review by management.

A bookkeeper is a type of translator between the owner and accountant. This person is the one most knowledgeable of the original entries that make up the Profit & Loss Statement, Balance Sheet, budgets and other financial documents pertaining to a company. Business owners usually are experts in their field, whether they are a doctor, an engineer, a graphic designer, a landscaper or any other career. That doesn't mean that they understand finance or even wish to! We act as a "translator" for many of our clients by taking the information requested and putting it into non-accounting terms that are understandable and can be related to their business.

There are different types of bookkeepers. You can hire full-time staff within your organization or you can outsource.

The level of expertise varies widely between bookkeepers, so it is important to determine your needs and start there. Some bookkeepers are very basic in their knowledge and performance. They take your source documents and post them into your accounting system with accuracy and efficiency and produce monthly statements. Some bookkeepers do the exact same thing, but ask thoughtful questions as they work. That bill went up this month, why was that? That credit card statement had a finance charge on it this month, why was that? The income number doesn't seem to match the amount of work going on in the office, what's going on? It is extremely important for you to determine your level of expertise needed for this area. A good high-level bookkeeper may be more expensive, but they can more than pay for themselves in what they can save you. They are looking to see what's happening around you financially, and they report it back to you.

CONTROLLERS/CFO (CHIEF FINANCIAL OFFICER)

All business owners need to understand their financial situation and if this book has not proven that, then we have not done our job. The financial level above your bookkeeper or office manager is a Controller/CFO. These folks help the owner steer the financial ship and are often more strategic in their thinking. They can prepare budgets and forecasts for the current and subsequent years, then help the owner review them on a monthly or quarterly basis to see where the business currently stands. A Controller/CFO can help prepare a business plan to help you get funding, can help determine the answers to those "What if" questions like buying or leasing a building, and when to add a new employee. They can help the owner calculate proper pricing strategies and review different scenarios of profit margins based on those strategies. They can analyze monthly or annual financial trends and prepare cash flow statements. Where the bookkeepers prepare a good accurate set of books, the Controller/CFO takes this information and looks at it in a more "big picture" strategic way in order to help you make good financial decisions.

Many of the examples we put in this book are stories of higher level financial analysis, i.e. something a Controller or CFO would do. If you don't think you can hire a full-time CFO, and many small business owners cannot, there are many Controller/CFOs out there that you can hire on a part-time or project basis. There are probably ones that even specialize in your industry, so take advantage of their expertise. Ask your current business network for referrals.

CPA OR TAX PREPARER

A good CPA is a huge wealth of knowledge and yet they are often so under-utilized. The two biggest pieces of advice we can give you are: first, turn your year-end papers in early and second, meet with your CPA during the off months. First, most of the time your tax preparer charges a flat fee for tax returns (or within a small range, depending on the work) so if you give them your information on February 1st or April 1st, while it won't make a difference to your fee necessarily, it will make a big difference in the amount of attention you receive. It's human nature and if you put yourself in their place for a moment you can completely understand why. If you turn your information in late, while your return will be done within the IRS rules, he or she may not have the time to ask and get questions answered which may influence your return. It might be so late that they make the most conservative assumptions based on what they see. And who can blame them? Of course they can file an extension, but sometimes that is a flag you may not want raised.

Allowing them to prepare your return early will give them the time they need to follow up on items that, if you were able to discuss, might allow them to use better actual information. And if we have not said it enough, documentation is a huge key here. If the CPA sees strong backup documentation, he can use more accurate actual numbers that might save you money on your return. If your bookkeeper has done their job, your tax information should be ready to be sent into the CPA or tax preparer usually around mid-February. Your information should be complete and should be accompanied with a cover letter/email noting any special occurrences or special notations you wish to bring to the CPA's attention.

Second, meet or speak with your CPA during the off season. Contact them before the year is over. Let them see where your financials currently are and discuss what you can do in order to put your company in the best tax light before the year closes. With many of our clients, we have meetings during Q4 to look at how the year is going to make some year-end purchase decisions or adjustments. Without updated, accurate information, these meetings would not take place or be fruitful.

Mary had an LLC and sent her CPA her financials quarterly. This helped her in two different ways. First, her CPA was able to adjust her quarterly tax payments according to her income. That way she was not overpaying the government her taxes during her quarterly payments thus preserving cash flow. Second, Mary was going to make a larger profit than expected for the year so her CPA suggested that she purchase the office equipment that she was planning on for next year in this current fiscal year instead. This increased her expenses thus reduced her income, thus reduced her tax burden for the year. She would have had the same situation if she had bought her equipment in the following year, but instead she was able to take advantage of accelerating her expense by a few months and reducing her tax burden in the current year.

There are other ways your CPA can help during the year that should be utilized. Would a 401k or a SEP or some other kind of pension plan work best for you? Maybe you want to know when to time your bonus. Maybe your business needs to purchase another vehicle. Should you buy it or lease it? Maybe you need more space for your business and have an opportunity to purchase a building. Should you buy the building or lease more space somewhere else, and if you do buy the building, what is the proper corporate structure in which to make the purchase? These are just some questions that can come up during the year where your CPA is the perfect place to start. If you feel like a number with your current CPA, find a new one, and the most expensive one isn't always the best. If your books are up to date and in good order, they can save you so much money that it could cover a good portion of their fees, and they have this knowledge at their fingertips.

Note: A tidbit about doing your own taxes – there are plenty of good tax preparation software programs currently on the market that are easy to use and come with guarantees. There is nothing wrong with using these services, but if you own a business, you need a partner to help you with that business, someone who can make suggestions and referrals, and you should be able to find that person without breaking the bank.

LAWYER

Having access to a good attorney on your team when you need one is also imperative. Depending on the type of business you have, you need to be able to call upon one for certain items related to your business. Once again, like your CPA, ask business associates and colleagues for referrals and check out their reputations and credentials. Attorneys usually specialize, so while you may need several different kinds of attorneys over the life of your business, if you find a good one, they are usually able to refer you to other good ones in different areas of the law or different areas of the country. The following are just a few things that a lawyer can assist you with:

BUSINESS AGREEMENT

If you have a partnership, it is wise to have an agreement. Putting together this agreement ahead of time could save you heartache and court costs later. These agreements usually cover how much each partner holds of the company and how to handle circumstances when or if they come up. There are so many unforeseen happenings in a single person owned business that when you partner with others, it's good to have a set of rules for these unforeseen happenings.

CONTRACTS WITH CLIENTS

Another agreement your attorney can help you with is the agreement with your clients. As long as the relationships with your clients are going along smoothly, everything is hunky-dory. These contracts are your livelihood and you want to be protected in case the relationship between you and a client goes sour. These contracts can cover you with regard to scope and deliverables, payment terms, proprietary information, and much more. Most of the time, business goes along without too many problems; you perform your service and you get paid on time. However, if something does go awry, you want a strong contract on your side.

COLLECTIONS

Your attorney can be invaluable in the area of collections as well. Let's say you have tried and tried to collect from a client, but to no avail. You are getting the runaround or perhaps they are avoiding you. There are several different avenues you can follow, depending on your business relationship, and a legal one exists as well. A strongly worded letter backed up by action can often correct a tipping boat. Your attorney may also know collection agencies or advise you on how to proceed through the small claims court system.

SUCCESSION PLANNING

Planning for the future of your company is also very important for any business, and you should begin planning well before you're gone. Determining your wishes for your company is one thing, but to make sure they are executed properly is another. Additionally, setting up buy/sell agreements between owners ahead of time is another way to keep the business running smoothly as changes take place.

FRANCHISING

Let's say you have built a business system that can be replicated over and over again with the same results and you are considering a franchising opportunity. An attorney can help you prepare the documents that not only protect your proprietary system, but also your income long into the future.

This handful of topics certainly does not exhaust the list of contracts and agreements your attorney can help you with. They can also help you with real estate closings or your own personal Will. Granted there are many examples of all of the types of agreements available for download and use on the internet; however, if you are not an expert, relying on the correct attorney will save you time and potentially headaches and money down the line. Hiring an attorney ahead of a problem is always far cheaper than hiring one after a problem.

INSURANCE AGENT

Insurance agents are often unsung heroes of your business. What they do is not glamorous and not on the front lines, and of course you hope you never need them, but when you do, if they are good they could save your business.

Different businesses need different insurances. Find an agent who is well versed in business insurances, not just home or auto, and take the time to discuss and answer their hundreds of questions. It's worth every minute. What types of insurance do you need? Retail stores have far different liability needs than a home office. Do you need general liability? Do you have a home office where you meet with clients? How about an overall umbrella policy? Do you have employees and if so, is your workers' compensation where it should be? Do you have a fiduciary responsibility to your clients? There's errors and omissions insurance, and maybe you need to be bonded as well. Directors and officer insurance is important for corporations, and you may need key officer and/or life insurance for yourself or certain employees. Some of these life insurance policies often fund the buy/sell agreements. Finally, don't forget disability, medical or dental insurance, if you choose to take it yourself or cover your employees.

Another insurance coverage that you or your business may need is special events coverage. How many golf outings have you been to where if you hit a hole in one on a specific hole you get a car? There is insurance for that! Non-profits sometimes have special circumstances which need to be covered differently as well.

Lastly, what is becoming more and more necessary is insurance for a cyber attack and/or data breach. Depending on your industry, this can also be the difference between being able to come back from such attacks or having to close your doors.

Find a good insurance agent and review with them all of your policies annually. It takes very little time and is a good business practice. The list seems to be endless, but a good insurance agent will only suggest the types of insurance you will need for your business and to safeguard your investment.

FINANCIAL ADVISOR

Many folks don't often speak to their financial advisor, maybe once a year if you're lucky. Once again, if that's all the communication you have with your advisor, you may be missing out on a good business source of information. Some folks inherited their advisors from their parents, some folks' investment companies have been bought and sold so many times that you may not know anyone at the current investment company. You need to meet your advisor and let them get to know you. A good financial advisor will ask you questions about what YOUR financial goals are then listen to you and understand your needs. It's a very personal, very fiduciary relationship and if you don't know who manages your money, it's time to find out.

A good financial advisor can help you start up your business. They may or may not be able to help you set up your business plan, but they certainly can review it with you and determine if you have the money to fund your business or if you need to go outside for financing. Whether you want to approve every minute detail of your investments or if you want to know nothing, you need to know your financial advisor, and if they are too busy or too hard to get a hold of, get a new one. Find an advisor who will strengthen your team, not just by managing your personal investments, but also by helping with your business. They need to understand your values and what is important to you. All investing decisions flow from this knowledge: reinvestment plans, 529 education plans and lending against assets all can and should flow from a talented and caring advisor.

BANKER

Your banker is another fiduciary relationship that can really make a difference to the day-to-day workings of your company. Before you open all your business accounts, determine which type of accounts you will need. Just checking? Checking and savings? Will you need an overdraft protection account or a line of credit? Will you need a large national bank or will you just need a regional or local bank? How much of a personal relationship will you need? Review their online banking if you'll be using that. There are all different types of accounts for all different types of businesses and all of these different types of accounts have different fees attached to them. Even if you have the same accounts for several years, the banks can change the requirements and fees and you can find yourself chasing refunds.

If you have a banker whom you know personally, you are ahead of the game. With some banks, every time you go into the branch the employees change and the person you opened your account with is no longer there or even at another branch in the same city. There are still some small regional or local banks where there is not such a revolving door. Find the best fit for you.

Note: Understand that some bankers are paid by the number of accounts they open and will want to have you open several. Be wary. Only open the accounts necessary for you. Too many accounts with too many minimums can lead to cash flow issues, higher bookkeeping fees and are just plain more work to maintain than they're worth. Be the same way with your credit cards. Keep only the ones you need. Annual fees will cost you. Credit limits can cost you. Once again, managing more than you need is just not worth the work.

CREDIT CARD MERCHANTS

Does your business take credit cards? You do not have to use your bank for your merchant processing, even though they may want you to. While it seems that everyone and their brother processes credit cards these days, there really are some great credit card processing companies out there, so ask around. A good credit card processing company will be able to look at your statements from the last couple of months and give you their fee structure without holding any information back. Be wary of folks promising you one thing and delivering another because this does happen. A good merchant processing company will also periodically monitor your transactions and review your history to ensure you are still saving the most money.

Chris ran a large car repair shop and did most of his business via credit card sales. His credit card company, as part of their service, was reviewing his history and saw a larger than normal refund rate (the computer system actually caught this for several months in a row). When they asked the owner about this, he didn't have an explanation. After some investigation, they were able to determine that most of the refunds were going to the same account, and after further investigation they determined that most of those refunds were done after a particularly heavy day of credit card sales. One of the office workers was processing refunds to her personal credit card and she had been doing this for a long time and was able to take thousands of dollars. It went unnoticed by the owner because it was after a large sales day and the amounts were small enough to justify. She was very clever in how she did this and would have continued to go undetected if the credit card company was not monitoring the account. Without a good credit card processing company, this would have continued and Chris would have lost even more money.

IT SUPPORT

Two recommendations on IT support. First, if you are not a technical company and are not able to handle your own IT needs in-house, have IT support just a phone call away. With everyone's reliance on their computers, you can be rendered completely useless if you lose a server, a modem goes down or a computer dies. Looking for IT support when you need it is too late. Set up your relationship ahead of time and, depending on your needs, determine if you need periodic support or just a dependable, helpful voice on the end of a phone in a crisis.

Second, if you are working with highly sensitive or confidential information as part of your business, it may be advantageous to have your computer set-up reviewed by a specialized IT security team. They can certainly advise you on password and server protection and encryption for your files and your computers. This can be a very prudent investment in today's environment.

Chapter 9

SOME PEOPLE STEAL

KEEPING A WATCHFUL EYE

Not everyone is dishonest, of course, most folks are far from it, but some people do have sticky fingers and do steal, so be careful who you have working in your business. In our business we can tell so many stories of theft and misappropriations, many more of which are in the newspaper every day. Every couple of months we get a new client simply because their prior bookkeeper, controller, treasurer, etc. stole from their business. And it doesn't stop with those who take care of your money either. Regular non-financial employees steal too. They can take inventory or they can steal time.

In this chapter we touch on areas to look out for, but it is by no means a complete list and nothing takes the place of you, as the business owner, checking up on things yourself.

BOOKKEEPERS AND TREASURERS

At the end of our client contracts we state that:

> "Stellar Support Associates, in the course of their work, will view and come into contact with confidential client information. All of us at Stellar Support Associates are fully committed to the utmost in client confidentiality and privacy. We are fully licensed and insured and most importantly, we know that our reputation for discretion is our most important asset."

And we mean it! It's one of the reasons we have been in business for so long and are recommended by current clients to new clients.

A bookkeeper or treasurer, whether a company employee or an outside contractor, really has nothing more than their reputation. When hiring, once again ask your colleagues for any referrals they may have, and whether you hire from a referral or not, check references. The trick to checking references is to make sure that there are no gaps in the résumé and check with each reference to determine the correct timeline. If there is a gap that cannot be adequately explained, let that be a red flag and move to the next candidate. Remember two things: these folks have access to all the information about your business you give them and there are some very sophisticated ways to steal these days.

If you are hiring an outside firm, make sure they are properly insured, are recommended or referred and have the expertise to help your business.

In one of our non-profit clients, the treasurer wanted to take a "loan" out for some personal expenses, but she didn't want to be so obvious about it. She was also in charge of payroll, so what she did was to overpay the president with a direct check for the same amount of her "loan" check, telling the president that she made an error in her pay and this check was the adjustment. She entered the president's check into the accounting system under Loan to Officer, just as hers was, so it looked like both of them took loans from the company. These loans sat out there for several years and were reported on the tax returns as though this was regular practice. It wasn't until she was let go for other misappropriations and we were brought in that we discovered what she had done. The president quickly paid back the "loan" and we cleared it from the books. The ex-treasurer filed bankruptcy within months of being dismissed and we found ourselves in a long line of other creditors and ultimately received nothing.

YOUR STAFF

There are many places to get potential employees and many of those include internet job searches. Many of our clients have had a lot of success online and will continue to do so. The obvious best way to protect yourself from hiring someone who may or may not work out with your company is to request, and then call, their references. Most of this is common sense and if your gut has helped you in the past, let it continue to guide you. These days there are also sophisticated background checks that can be done that include their presence on the internet.

Getting back to an earlier point, staff can take your time and your money. If you have been prudent with how you secure your inventory, as we have already talked about, and how you secure your cash, which we are about to talk about, the only other thing your employee can steal is your time.

Is your employee working all the hours they say they are? Here, incorporating a time clock system can help. The first type is the old-fashioned punch-in and punch-out time clock. It's been around the longest and is still one of the best and simplest ways for employees to track how many hours they are there working. Next is a virtual time clock that they log into from their computer. When they sit down at their desk, they simply log in, work their day, then log out in the end. This works well even for employees on salary as just a simple way to keep track of what days they worked. A third way is for employees to log their time by job or task. For a professional company, this is the most useful. On a daily or no more than weekly basis, employees track their time, usually in an online system, by whose job or which task they were working on. This provides two things: it shows the actual hours by day of what they worked and it helps manage the hours spent on each job to show efficiency, as we saw in an earlier chapter.

INTERNAL CONTROLS

There are many small systems that can be put into place to help protect your company information and assets. Once again, most are common sense, and this list is by no means a complete list! These are just a few of the basics we find with many of our clients. We know that small businesses have to rely on a small number of people (sometimes just one!) to wear many different hats, and this makes some internal controls difficult to manage. We know this can also be a difficult balancing act. Some business owners feel the need to control every aspect of their business and this can slow their profitability and their growth, and on the opposite end, some business owners want to see nothing and completely trust their employees and this can open them up to possible improprieties. There needs to be a balance for a company to run well, so look around your company, look at every little task, every little area of exposure, and do your best to put controls into place that can protect you without overworking you.

WHO HAS ACCESS TO WHAT?

The most obvious is online banking. Everyone uses it now, so who has the user name and password? Each person who has access should have their own username and password so there is a record of what each person is doing if you ever need it. Many banks can give online access to employees with certain limits. Employees can set up payments, for example, but the approval must come from a second person. Or each employee has a limit on the dollar amount of certain transactions. The same goes for your credit card or merchant banking accounts as well. Find your level of comfort and implement your online systems to reflect that. Lastly, are your personal accounts and business accounts under the same online access? It would be prudent to separate these accounts online to limit your employees from not just having access to make transactions from those accounts but also it's none of their business. We know all of this might be additional hassle on the front end, but think of it as insurance we spoke about earlier. It's better to be safe than sorry.

SAFEGUARDING YOUR FILES

Companies can also have files with sensitive employee or customer information in them, social security numbers, credit reports, credit card numbers, etc., and they need to be safeguarded. Where are these files located and how are they locked up? Are they open and accessible during the day and by whom? Who has the keys, both during the day and after close of business?

There are company desks with confidential company information in them as well, such as payroll information and bank statements. Are these desks locked at night as well? And who has those keys?

MONEY COMING IN

Fewer and fewer companies are dealing in actual cash these days and that is good for accounting; however, the mail at some companies is filled with checks from clients, and they still do get some cash. These need to be received into your system completely and correctly. In an ideal world, you would have two people opening the mail and signing off that a check or cash was received and that it was posted to a customer's account. However, in the real world where we are doing more work with fewer employees, you have a couple of good options. If you have a lot of payments received in the mail, you can buy a lockbox service usually at your bank, where all the payments are sent to your bank and they have the internal controls to process the payments and put the funds directly into your account. This service does cost money, but if this sounds like it might work for you, then look into it. The second option is simpler, yet effective if done properly.

Bruce ran a large car dealership, and while he played a lot of golf, almost every day he would be at the store and open the mail. When the pile of mail came in the morning, often wrapped up in several rubber bands by the post office, the office manager would set the whole pile on his desk and wait for him to go through it. It was a treasure trove of information for Bruce, this simple exercise. First, he would see what checks came in for the day and he would write them down on a notepad he kept by his desk. The next day, to make sure that the deposit going off to the bank included each of them he would compare his notepad to the deposit slip. He would go over all his bank statements and credit card statements at this time too, to make sure he knew what all the entries were, and he would circle some of them and ask the office manager to provide him with the backup for certain purchases. Here's the key, he would circle some even if he KNEW what they were.

This exercise allowed him to make sure that his office was documenting expenses properly and would let them know he was watching. He was able to see if vendor bills were correct right away, and if it needed his attention, he would address it immediately instead of waiting for the process to take over. He saw all the sales circulars and looked for new ideas, he saw all the letters from the factory right away, and of course he saw all the junk mail. Sometimes he would find mail in there addressed to his employees, some even had items of personal mail sent to the dealership such as bank or credit card statements. Sometimes employees asked ahead of time if this was okay with him to use their business address for personal mail, and sometimes they wouldn't. This helped him gain insight into his employees and maybe keep an eye on them. Lastly, and this is the best part, sometimes Bruce didn't come in, or even if he did, he wouldn't touch the mail and just hand it back to the office manager for her to process. It is such a simple system, yet so very effective.

MONEY GOING OUT

For business owners, usually they are the only person who has the ability to sign checks and this works just fine. Perhaps the owner's immediate family has the ability as well, if that works logistically. There are circumstances when requiring two signatures on a check is a better idea. If the company is large with many different areas, requiring the double signature puts into place a control so that no one person has access to all of the funds without oversight. The other circumstance when two signatures are prudent is when there is no single "business owner" such as non-profit organizations. Just like with large companies, this does not give access of the organization's funds to just one person. There is an extra fiduciary responsibility non-profits have to their donors, so a double signature increases accountability and transparency to those outside the organization.

Having said all this about check-signing ability, the fact is that there is no substitute for you, as the business owner, to review the bank statements and credit card statements yourself every month. If this is not possible, then make spot checks but do them as often as possible. It would also be prudent for each invoice to be "approved" by the owner before it is paid or if that is too cumbersome, for a list of open accounts payable to be provided to the owner prior to checks being written. These steps don't take a lot of time, but could save you a lot of headache later.

Let's look at a quick bill pay procedure in action. When an invoice is received in the mail at Martin & Brenner CPA firm, the office manager needs to get approval from the managing partner for processing the payment. After getting her sign-off, the invoice is entered into the accounting system along with the date it's due and then the hardcopy of the invoice is placed into a tickler file by date to be paid at the appropriate time with a check signed by a different partner than the one who approved it. This does two things: first, this allows the firm to manage when it pays its bills thereby monitoring optimum cash flow; second, because one partner approves an invoice and another signs the check, there are two sets of eyes to look at each invoice, thus satisfying internal control procedures.

Credit card refunds need to be treated just like checks going out. There should be an additional level of approval before one can be processed and that can be as simple as having a second employee approve the process or as detailed as having you approve each one. As we saw in Chris's automotive business earlier, refunds are the same as cash and can be manipulated, especially if there are large numbers of both charges and refunds.

Approval of expenses is also something that can reduce your chance of misappropriation of funds. In certain organizations, having expense reports prepared in order to get checks cut, and then having those expense reports approved by a second person, usually a manager, helps to eliminate bogus expenses. These expense reports should be accompanied by the appropriate receipts to prove the charge. Many companies require pre-approval of outside expenses and that helps too. If you don't have an expense report form for your business, there are many examples on the internet to start with and make your own.

SEPARATION OF DUTIES

While you cannot usually stop collusion between two employees, separating certain duties in a company is sometimes the best way to slow it way down. If you have the luxury of having one person open the mail, another post payments to customers, and yet another make the deposits, that will help. Also, if the person placing the equipment order is not the same person receiving the equipment order, that is good too. Many small businesses don't have this luxury so you must be aware. Many small companies have employees doing many, if not all, of the duties and perhaps have been working for them many years.

While this does bring some comfort, of course it is not foolproof and so, as a business owner, you need to be aware that sometimes even those closest to us can deceive us. Keep an eye out for subtle things as well as obvious things. Look and listen for changes to your employees. Perhaps personal issues, financial issues, and family problems are creeping up. Did they show up with a brand new car way out of their price range? Opulent vacations? Other large purchases? We don't mean to make you paranoid, but keep a diligent eye on your employees. Or maybe have their managers do it. Look for opportunities to separate duties, especially those duties surrounding money and inventory.

SAFEGUARDING YOUR ASSETS

Is your company inventory and equipment locked up? Is only one person responsible for it? Are there sign-outs required? What happens to outdated or obsolete inventory?

Karl had a large warehouse in his back office full of audio/visual inventory waiting to be installed on jobs, and sometimes, as happens with electronics, this inventory would become obsolete overnight and couldn't be used on the project it was originally intended for. In theory, if an item became obsolete, an effort would be made immediately to try to return it to the manufacturer for credit. In practice however, even with current jobs, this didn't happen. One day Karl was on eBay looking for a specific piece of older electronic equipment to match a client's older system, when he saw what looked like some of his own inventory being sold there. When he looked further into it, he found out that one of his designers, who had access to the open inventory, had taken some obsolete equipment (DVDs, speakers, older generation iPads, etc.) home and began selling them online as extra income for himself.

For inventory, we talked about the importance of doing a total inventory count as often as feasible, certainly annually, but keeping an up-to-date list and doing spot checks monthly, or as often as needed, is very important to safeguarding your assets.

Another Big Fat Disclaimer: Please understand that this list of internal controls is in no way complete, and should not be solely relied on to protect everything in your business. But do know that theft does occur, by all kinds of people and in many different ways. The majority of people are honest, hard-working individuals. However, there is always that one "bad apple" that ruins the bunch. As business owners, we just need to be constantly vigilant and observant to weed out those "bad apples" for the health of our businesses.

One final word on internal controls. So much of strong internal controls is perception. As the owner, you probably do not have the time to monitor all these different areas all at the same time. However, if your employees know that you *could* monitor a certain area, and often do at certain intervals, they are less likely to try to steal from you. If they *perceive* that you are keeping an eye on them and that they could be caught at any time, they are less likely to try anything below board. Sometimes doing just enough to give the impression you are watching everything is all that is needed.

CONCLUSION

In our favorite bullet form!

- Start by asking yourself the difficult business questions, and if you cannot find answers, hire someone who can. No one expects you to know all the answers and sometimes the best knowledge is to know where your business intelligence stops and when it's time to ask for help.

- Know where your money is. Know why you need strong accurate financials and give your bookkeeper the tools and access to what they need to do a good job for you.

- Get your act together and set up your systems for documenting and filing. Make sure you have all of the backup for all of your transactions in an organized easy-to-reach place if you need them and keep one fiscal year together at a time.

- Have an accurate set of meaningful financial statements. If you don't like or don't understand how the statements are set up or what they tell you, have them prepared differently and know which reports you want to look at every month or quarter or year. You'll start to spot trends when they are in the beginning stages and begin to make smart business decisions.

- Make sure you bill your clients on a consistent basis and in the proper manner. Understand what can happen if you do not stay on top of your billing and vow not to let that happen in your business.

- Collect your receivables and monitor your cash flow so that you can pay your bills in full and on time.

- Set up a yearly budget and longer term forecast for your business. Make your assumptions as accurate as possible based on your current market knowledge and then monitor your monthly actuals against your current budget and annual forecast.

- Your people are your most important asset. Set up the structure of your company based on what duties need to be performed and then fill each job with a qualified strong candidate. Ensure that each of your employees has a job description and that there exist procedures to follow for any job in the company in case of personnel changes.

- Build your strong business support team by asking for referrals from your business network. Each of these folks brings something to the table that will help you run your business. Check references, reputations and licensing requirements if applicable.

- Remember that some people do take advantage of situations. Put in controls and safeguards to minimize any theft of money, inventory or time. Remember that the perception that you are watching goes a long way even if you aren't watching every single day.

- Lastly, run a PROACTIVE company, not a REACTIVE one. Your bottom line will be healthier and your headaches reduced.

We hope that this book has helped you understand the financial systems of your business better and can assist you in many different areas. If there is anything we can help you with, please don't hesitate to contact us at michele.johnson@stellarsa.com and lorraine.kennedy@stellarsa.com.

We wish you all financial success.

GLOSSARY

Accounts payable – Individuals or companies to whom you owe money

Accounts receivable – What a client owes you for goods or services rendered

Aging of accounts receivable – A list of which clients owe you how much money and for how long they have owed it

Annual retention file – A file of all relevant accounting information for a specific year, and only that year

Asset – Items in a business that have monetary value

Balance Sheet – A statement showing the assets, liabilities and owner's equity of a business entity at a specific date in time

Bill payment procedure – A set of steps implemented in order to pay an invoice utilizing proper internal controls

Chart of accounts – List of accounts by title and/or number for a business

Check register – The list of each check a company has written, the date it was written and to whom it was written

Credit terms – 2%/10, net 30 – Payment terms such that if you pay the invoice off within 10 days you can receive a 2% discount, otherwise you pay the total in 30 days

Current assets – Assets which are able to be turned into cash quickly

Fiscal year – The 12 months which constitute a company's "year". Usually January to December, but can also be any other 12 month period

Furniture and fixtures – Long-term assets owned by a company. They are usually depreciated over 5, 10 or 20 years

General Journal entry – The original entry for accounting data. The transaction includes date, description, debit amount and account and credit amount and account

Liability – Amounts owed to outsiders

Line of credit – Usually a bank offered amount of money a person or company can borrow against

Inventory – The materials a business purchases or produces for sale to its customers

Owner's equity – The financial interest of the owners of a business

Profit & Loss Statement – A statement covering a period of time registering the net profit of a company

Profit margin – The ratio of profits earned to total costs, over a certain period of time

Purchase order – A promise to pay given to a vendor in exchange for products or services

Trial balance – A report that compares the total of all debit balances with the total of all credit balances

Vendor – A person or company from which you purchase assets or materials in order to produce income

ABOUT THE AUTHORS

Michele Johnson and Lorraine Kennedy are partners in Stellar Support Associates in Westport, CT.

Stellar Support Associates provides bookkeeping, CFO services and business consulting for many small businesses and individuals in Connecticut and New York, as well as nationwide and internationally.

Michele Johnson has a B.S. in Accounting from the University of North Carolina at Greensboro and an M.B.A. from Indiana University. She worked as an internal auditor for a large regional bank in Charlotte, NC, on the corporate finance staff of Chrysler Corporation, and was the General Manager of a 5 Star Dodge dealership in Detroit, MI. She has been offering bookkeeping and financial analysis services to clients since 2005.

Lorraine Kennedy has a B.S. in Business and an M.A.T. in Education from Sacred Heart University in Fairfield, CT. She began her professional career at GE Capital in the financial marketing sector, spent time with GTE (now Verizon) in marketing and has worked with small and medium sized companies in marketing and mergers and acquisitions. Lorraine established Support Plus in 1990 also providing bookkeeping and management services.

Between us we have over 40 years of financial consulting experience and have helped scores of clients become more financially fit and independent. We hope that this book will help achieve those same goals for you.

www.stellarsa.com

22776562R00072

Printed in Great Britain
by Amazon